HAUNTED
MONTGOMERY,
ALABAMA

HAUNTED MONTGOMERY, ALABAMA

FAITH SERAFIN

Haunted
America

Published by Haunted America
A Division of The History Press
Charleston, SC 29403
www.historypress.net

Unless otherwise noted, all images appear courtesy of the author.

First published 2013

Manufactured in the United States

ISBN 978.1.60949.930.3

Library of Congress Cataloging-in-Publication Data

Serafin, Faith.
Haunted Montgomery, Alabama / Faith Serafin.
pages cm. --ˈ(Haunted America)
ISBN 978-1-60949-930-3 (pbk.)
1. Ghosts--Alabama--Montgomery. 2. Haunted places--Alabama--Montgomery. I. Title.
BF1472.U6S435 2013
133.109761'47--dc23
2013031637

You don't need to believe in ghosts to enjoy a good ghost story.
—*Kathryn Tucker Windham*

CONTENTS

ACKNOWLEDGEMENTS

This literary adventure has brought a great number of people I would like to acknowledge and give credit to. While researching and writing this book, I was introduced to some very informative and highly educated people in the area of history, legends, folklore and, of course, ghost stories from Montgomery. I have been fortunate to have had the time to personally interview and have countless conversations with many of them. First, I would like to give a great deal of credit to my friend Shannon Fontaine. Shannon is the nightly chauffeur and owner of the Haunted Hearse Tours–Montgomery. Shannon's knowledge of ghost stories in many of the capital city's most historical locations helped to inspire several of the stories featured in *Haunted Montgomery, Alabama*. Mary Ann Neeley's contributions helped establish the history of these stories with great accuracy, and Willie Thompson of the Scott and Zelda Fitzgerald Museum, who gave an inspiring interview regarding the wandering spirit of Zelda Fitzgerald.

I would like to personally thank Mr. Eric A. Kidwell, director of the Houghton Memorial Library at Huntingdon College for his interview and information about the library ghost and for his generosity in allowing me to photograph the location. I would also like to thank the countless students at Huntingdon who shared their personal experiences about the campus spirits. I'd also like to recognize those who have anonymously contributed to this book, and I must also thank the ghost of Hank Williams, who, in a dream, informed me that I should be the one to write his ghost story. Also, I must give credit to my daughters, Tori and Jordis, who spent countless hours with me, scouring over dusty records in the Alabama State Archives and to my sons Jason, Jared and Eric for helping me in my seemingly endless cemetery searches and haunted outings.

I was also very fortunate to be able to work with other great authors and paranormal investigators from Alabama on their History Press projects this year. David Higdon and Brett Talley's *Haunted Alabama Black Belt*; Michelle Smith's *Legends, Lore and True Tales of the Chattahoochee*; *Haunted Shelby County, Alabama* by Kim Johnston; and *Haunted South Alabama* by Jessica Penot. As always, I must express my gratitude to my team of paranormal investigators and researchers, the Alabama Paranormal Research Team. Their dedication and devotion to the paranormal has helped fuel many of the books I have written and, hopefully, will continue to write.

And last but not least, I must thank my family for all their patience and understanding while writing for the "Haunted America" series and my very supportive and loving husband, Tony. He has supported and helped me focus on my goals, which motivates me to write more on the supernatural and document any and all paranormal occurrences I can.

INTRODUCTION

In July 2012, I traveled to Nashville, Tennessee, with my very dear friend Nicola Hampsey of Basingstoke, England. We planned the trip after a series of unusual dreams led me to seek out the ghost of Hank Williams. While attending the Nashville Ghost Tours, I spoke briefly with the tour guide about sightings of Hank Williams's ghost. Nicola and I were informed that his spirit is most often seen leaving the back of the Ryman Theater, and at the conclusion of the tour, which was conveniently at the Ryman Theater, our curiosity led us to an alleyway that connects the back of the old theater and the party district on Broadway.

As I stood there in the alley, it began to thunder and lightning flashed across the sky. It started to rain, and I thought about the recurring dreams I had that led me here. In these dreams, a thunderstorm drives me into an old cemetery in Montgomery, Alabama, and an apparition appears to me at the grave of Hank Williams. The sound of a match being lit sparks my attention as a tall, slender man, silhouetted against the night sky, appears. Although I cannot see his face, the dull glow from his lit cigarette and strong southern accent seem to make me vaguely familiar with him. "Are you the lady writin' them ghost books in Alabama?" he says. "Yes sir, I have written one or two," I answer. "Well honey, when you get ready, I want you to write my ghost story." Realizing, at this point, I am in the ghostly presence of a legendary man, I reply, "Yes, sir! I'd be honored to write about you, Mr. Williams." A haunting smile comes over the figure's face as he says, "I'll be waitin'." The apparition fades away as he walks among the headstones.

We didn't find the ghost of Hank Williams that night in the alley behind the Ryman, but we did have an experience neither of us would ever forget. As we stood there, soaked to the bone, Nicola and I were flabbergasted when we saw English rocker and original member of the Beatles Ringo Star exit the theater through the crowd. He had just finished a performance at the Ryman and was in Nashville celebrating his seventy-second birthday that weekend. We came to Nashville to find a legendary ghost and instead found a living legend.

Though Nashville, Tennessee, is located nearly 280 miles north of Montgomery, Alabama, this was the location and the experience that inspired my first story for *Haunted Montgomery, Alabama*. Many historic people, legendary events and unusual and captivating tales can be told as part of the darker side of Montgomery's history. The heart of Dixie is still very much alive with the spirits of yesterday, and they are still reaching out to tell their stories, from Prattville to Montgomery, history is resurrected in the stories of Indian folklore, Civil War heroes, disastrous events and the legacies of those individuals who have helped to cultivate the ghost stories of this city's historic locations. They can all be found in this small collection of mysterious stories.

MONTGOMERY GHOSTS

THE MANY GHOSTS OF
HANK WILLIAMS

There are many ghostly tales from the state of Alabama, from Sloss Furances in Birmingham to the Civil War dead of Fort Morgan in Gulf Shores. The list of ghost stories and haunted locations are endless, but there is one legendary spirit bound to so many locations in the state and abroad that they all lay claim to his ghosts.

Hiram King Williams was born September 17, 1923, in Butler County, Alabama. His parents, Elonzo "Lon" Huble Williams and Jessie Lilybelle "Lily" Skipper-Williams, were both hard-working people who made their living working in the logging camps that traveled along America's railway systems. Just before Hiram was born, his father, Lon, joined the army near the end of World War I and was shipped from Camp Shelby in Mississippi and then to France with the 113th Regiment of Engineers, 42nd Division. During this time, he sustained a head injury that was not received in combat. Allegedly he had fallen from a truck while hauling rocks, but his family later noted that he may have been injured while fighting over a young French girl. Lily Williams was a very formidable woman. She was of large stature with broad shoulders and had a very strict and no-nonsense personality. She also worked very hard alongside her husband in the logging camps, and after many years of traveling and living in box cars and railroad shacks, they rented the Old Kendrick place in Butler County, where Lilly worked on a small strawberry farm and ran a store out of one end of their home.

Hiram, from birth, was a lively and joyful child. However, he suffered a severe handicap that was not diagnosable at the time. In his early childhood, he didn't participate in sports or anything physically active. His parents knew at birth that he had an unusual knot on his spine, which today would have been determined to be spina bifida occulta, which is a condition that causes the nerves in the spinal column to be damaged by defects in the bones, structure of the spine or damage to the nerve endings in the spinal column. This caused him a great deal of pain and meant he could not participate in sports or heavy physical activity. His condition most likely contributed to his interest in music at a very young age and his mother noted in his first biography that he would sit with her in church at the piano and sing so loudly that he annoyed the other churchgoers. Hiram loved music above all other activities, and this was the beginning of his short but influential career in country music.

Sometime during September 1929, when Hiram was six, his father's brain injury affected his ability to smile and blink. The following January, Lily took Lon to the Veterans Hospital in Pensacola, Florida. He was later sent to Alexandria, Louisiana, where he stayed until 1937. During this time little Hiram grew isolated without his father and it impacted him greatly. His emotional burden concerning his missing father was obvious in one of his earliest unpublished songs, "I Wish I Had a Dad." It was rumored that Lily led most people to believe that Lon was dead during this time, stating that he was gassed and shell-shocked during his time in the war.

In Lon's absence, Lily moved her family to Georgiana, near Highway 31, where they rented a small log cabin, which burned down shortly after they moved in. This left her family penniless and without any possessions, but she loaded her children into a wagon and started for town in search of a new home. Lily was stopped by a local man named Thaddeus B. Rose, who offered to allow her and the children to stay in a home he owned at 127 Rose Avenue, free of charge, until she could get back on her feet. Though proud, Lily accepted the offer and moved in. Neighbors helped out by bringing in meals to the Williamses and lending them what they could spare in household goods and donated clothes.

During this time, Lily took on family members who needed to be cared for in exchange for money. She also worked in a local convalescent hospital for a while to bring in extra income for her family. Hiram's ever-growing obsession with music was definitely encouraged by his mother and sisters. Lily even took on overnight duties at the convalescent hospital to send him to a school in Avant, Alabama, where he learned to sing Bible hymns. He was particularly fond of black church music and favored the harmonic and orchestrated rhythms.

When Hiram was almost eleven years old, he met a local street musician named Rufus Payne. He was a slender-built black man who always carried a spiked vessel of tea, earning him the nickname, "Tee-Tot." Rufus "Tee-Tot" Payne had been born to slave parents on the Payne Plantation in Lowndes County. At some point, the Payne family moved to New Orleans, Louisiana, and Rufus was influenced by the jazz music and soulful culture of the city. Later, Tee-Tot played on the streets of Georgiana. While he was performing as a one-man band (playing cymbals tied between his knees while strumming the guitar or harp), children took a curious interest in him, and they frequently harassed Tee-Tot for lessons. Hiram was one of those children, and Tee-Tot taught him everything he could.

After 1936, Lily Williams opened a downtown boardinghouse on South Perry Street in Montgomery, Alabama. Hiram was sixteen, and just like Tee-Tot, he played his guitar on the streets of Montgomery while singing and selling peanuts. Lily had managed to contribute to his musical interests by buying him a guitar on Christmas in 1937. She knew he could become a great musician if she could get him recognized by local radio personalities, and she entered him in many talent shows around Montgomery. His first was at the Empire Theater Friday Night Talent Show, where he won the fifteen-dollar grand prize. He later won so many of the talent shows that management at the Empire actually asked him to stop performing.

Hiram decided to drop his given name in favor of "Hank" and met Braxton Schuffert, a singer and songwriter and substantial connection in radio at WSFA. Hank preformed for Braxton, and eventually a feature segment for Hank, known as the "Singing Kid," became part of Schuffert's weekly broadcast. He later paired up with a local musician and fiddle player named Freddy Beach. "Dad" Crysel organized small talent shows in a hall on Commerce Street in Montgomery where Freddy and Hank played on a weekly basis. Braxton's show would eventually bring Smith "Hezzy" Adair to meet Hank Williams, and he helped organize Hank's first band, the Drifting Cowboys, and in 1938, Hank dropped out of school permanently to work as a full-time performer.

In early 1940, Hank met Roy Acuff, the famed Western singer and performer who abandoned his first band, the Crazy Tennesseans, after he joined the Grand Ole Opry in 1938. Roy Acuff would help bring Hank further up the country music ladder by acting as his publisher. Hank also went on a brief tour with Juan Lobo, also known as "Jack

Wolf," a cowboy entertainer who performed western gun shticks and sold handmade chaps and belts. Braxton would eventually leave the band, but Hank and his Drifting Cowboys continued to travel and perform all over Alabama, Georgia and Florida, acquiring different band members who seemed almost disposable at this point in Hank's career. Hank was gaining the respect of many prominent people in country music, but he was at odds with his band members over his excessive alcohol abuse, which greatly hindered his performances.

Hank was now becoming a well-known prodigy in the music industry, and though he was determined to make it to the top, he harbored some demons that would come back to haunt him on many occasions throughout his lifetime. Hank traveled extensively with the Drifting Cowboys and eventually met Audrey Sheppard. He was working a medicine show in Banks, Alabama, when they met. Medicine shows were a clever ploy to sell medicinal herbs and "snake oil" for household purposes and home remedies. Hank immediately fell in love with Audrey, and within several months of their first meeting, they were living together and traveling with the band.

Audrey came to understand, just as Hank's band members did, that he had a substantial problem with alcohol. Hank didn't drink all the time, but when he did, he drank himself into a severe state of depression and sometimes anger. He struggled throughout his career to keep musicians in his band due to his inability to control this debilitating habit. However, it was the easiest way for him to cope with his business and personal relationships. He also developed some dependency to painkillers later on in life because of problems with his failing back.

Though Audrey loved Hank with all her heart, she refused to marry him until he had spent a year sober. Frequently they separated during their relationship due to his outbursts when intoxicated. While living in Andalusia, Alabama, where Hank and Audrey were married on December 15, 1944, Hank was locked up and charged with disorderly conduct after a domestic dispute broke out between them. Hank went on a drinking binge and threw her out with all her clothes. He was arrested that evening and spent the night in the Andalusia jail. Audrey sent band member Don Helms to bail him out the next day. Helms reported he was embarrassed to have to go and get Hank out of jail, but he paid the thirty dollars to get him out. While inside the jail, Helms looked across the way at Hank sitting on a bench in his cell. Hank glared back at him and said, "What d'ya want me to do? Stand on my head?" Hank was sober enough, but his defiance was still very profound. On the way out, one of the jailers said, "Come back and see us, Hank." Hank replied, "All of you can go to hell!"

This was a time in Hank's life when his drunken antics would cost him greatly in many areas of his personal life and career, but it still molded his music and the heartfelt emotions he poured into all the lyrics he wrote. Hank's music was written from the pages of his life and, most of all, from his heart. Some of the songs he wrote, like "Mother is Gone," "My Darling Baby Girl," "A Tramp on the Street" and "I Wish I Could Forget," were all indicative of his struggles up to this point in his life.

Hank had been denied a place on the cast of the Grand Old Opry because of his alcoholism, but Audrey approached Fred Rose, the president of Acuff-Rose Music, while in Nashville, Tennessee, and Rose signed Hank to a contract with Sterling Records. In September 1946, a six-song record, including "Never Again" and "Honkey Tonkin'," gained the attention of MGM, and he signed with them in 1947. He released "Move It on Over," a major hit that sent him to Shreveport, Louisiana, where he joined the radio show *The Louisiana Hay Ride*.

This was the pivotal point in Hank's career that sent him from mainstream radio into the limelight as one of America's most prominent and famous country music singers and performers. On May 26, 1949, Hank's son, Randal Hank Williams Jr., was born, and the following month on June 11, Hank finally made his debut at the Grand Old Opry in Nashville. Hank, despite his pitfalls, had successfully reached the peak of his glory and was a devoted and successful musician and performer. He continued to write and preform new hits like "Nobody's Lonesome for Me," "Moaning the Blues," "Cold Cold Heart" and "My Buckets Got a Hole In It." Everything seemed to be in perfect order, but once again, Hank's dark side would cause him to face more challenges.

Hank suffered a substantial injury during a hunting trip that subsequently aggravated his fragile back condition, and within a few short months, he was drinking heavily again. Hank also became addicted to the morphine that he took to ease his chronic back pain, and in 1952, his beloved Audrey divorced him. In August of that same year, he was fired from the Opry.

Hank went back to radio for a while, but in the words of "Ballad of Hank Williams," written by his son, Hank Williams Jr., and his friend Don Helms, "Hank run through a fifty and he run through a hundred and he run through a thousand just as hard as he could go," spending money hand over fist. He was drinking excessively, and along with his morphine habit, Hank was slowly killing himself and his career. Hank moved back in with his mother, Lily, and continued recording music. "Jambalaya" and "Settin' the Woods on Fire" were chart toppers even in his state of physical and mental distress.

Hank had always been very much a ladies man, and it was rumored that women would actually faint in the presence of him while performing. In the fall of 1952, Hank married Billie Jean Jones in New Orleans at a paid event where tickets were sold to attend the wedding. Hank and Billie's relationship was as rocky, if not worse, than Hank's previous marriage. On December 28, 1952, Hank gave his last performance in Montgomery, Alabama, at the Elite Café at the eighth-annual party of the American Federation of Musicians Local 479, and the next day, Billie Jean left him after a heated argument. He had a short-term relationship with Bobbie Jett prior to his short marriage to Billie Jean that resulted in his daughter, Jett Williams, who was born January 6, 1953 (six days after his death). During this time, he also recorded "Kaw-Liga," "Your Cheating Heart" and "Take These Chains." These were to be his last recording sessions.

While en route to a show in West Virginia, Hank had taken to heavy drinking and had also visited a doctor that same day for a shot of morphine to help his back through the long car ride. Hank and the driver, Charles Carr, a local college student hired to drive Hank to his shows, stopped several times on the journey. Shortly after midnight on January 1, 1943, when they pulled into a gas station in Oak Hill, Virginia, Hank was unresponsive in the back seat. He was dead.

On January 4, 1953, the largest funeral in Alabama history took place at the Montgomery Auditorium. Nearly thirty thousand spectators and mourners paid their final respects to the legend that was Hank Williams. One of his last recordings, conveniently labeled "I'll Never Get Out of this World Alive," was released just after his death and was a haunting and chilling reminder of his untimely death.

Though his life painted a flamboyant and sometimes chaotic picture, Hank's spirit today is just as popular as he was during his lifetime. Many locations, from Alabama to Tennessee, lay claim to Luke the Drifter's ghost. Songs by country music superstars David Allan Coe and Alan Jackson tell stories of supernatural experiences involving the ghost of Hank Williams. Even Hank's son, Hank Williams Jr., and grandson Shelton Hank Williams III have songs regarding his childhood home in Georgiana and his grave site in the Oakwood Annex Cemetery in Montgomery.

David Allan Coe's song "The Ride" tells of a chilling encounter with a pale stranger who stops to pick him up in an antique Cadillac while hitchhiking to Nashville. The stranger offers him a ride and some advice, "If you're big star bound, let me warn ya', it's a long, hard ride." Alan Jackson's song about Hank Williams, "Midnight in Montgomery," tells a similar experience when he stopped to pay his respects at the grave of Hank Williams and the apparition of a "drunk man in a cowboy hat" took him by surprise. He describes the apparition as "wearing shiny boots, a Nudi suit and haunting, haunted eyes." Hank's son, Hank Jr., may have the best description of a spiritual encounter in his song "127 Rose Avenue." Regarding the spirit that lingers in the boyhood home of Hank Williams in Georgiana, the song

Eric Serafin poses at the grave of Hank Williams in Montgomery, Alabama. *Costume Courtesy of Ryan Fontaine.*

describes a "sad-eyed boy, with his guitar, cutting his teeth on the blues," and the chorus continues with "caretaker said as he shook his head, son do you believe in ghosts? For a five-dollar bill, you can feel the chill that he felt long ago." Hank Jr. also lets the listener know that he himself has felt an overwhelming presence of his father in the home while on a tour there.

Not far from Georgiana, in Andalusia, Alabama, the Old Andalusia Jail also possesses some residual and intelligent activity associated with the ghost of Hank Williams. The Alabama Paranormal Research Team conducted a paranormal investigation at the location in October 2010, alongside the Andalusia Police Department. During the investigation, we found that some of the spirits of the old jail still find comfort in having visitors. Several EVPs (electronic voice phenomenon) were recorded on digital recorders of slamming cell doors and disembodied voices. But the shadowy figure of a very thin man was seen in one of the upstairs cells where Hank spent the night. Several members of the team experienced the movement of this shadowy presence that night and also documented the sound of footsteps as the entity seemed to follow us during the investigation. One EVP collected that night was a simple answer to whether Hank's spirit was there. While investigating the jail, I asked the question, "Do you like having visitors?" the reply was simple, "Yup." This was a hair-raising experience and a possible indication that Hank's remarks to the jailer all those years ago may have been a threat he intends to fulfill, even from beyond his grave.

The Elite Café in Montgomery, where Hank held his last performance, has also yielded some interesting paranormal activity. It was investigated by local ghost hunters who witnessed a chair move on its own. Others say his spirit travels as far away as Nashville, Tennessee, to the Ryman Auditorium, the original location of the Grand Ole Opry from 1943 to 1974. It's rumored and attested to on local ghost tours put on by the Nashville Ghost Tours that Hank Williams's ghost is seen leaving the back of the theater, in the alley.

The possibilities of Hank Williams rambling spirits are endless. It's appropriate that two separate highways located near Montgomery and Georgiana are dedicated to him. These lost highways are still haunted with the memories and legacy of the man Hank Williams and of his spirit. The reminders of his influence can be found all over the world of country music, even though his life was cut tragically short. The spirit of Hank Williams lives on through song and inspiration, somewhere between raising hell and amazing grace.

HAUNTED HUNTINGDON COLLEGE

NOT JUST THE RED LADY

Prior to the Civil War, Huntingdon College was located in Tuskegee, Alabama, under its original name, Tuskegee Female College. Doctor Andrew Adgate Lipscomb was the first president of the institution, which opened to female students on February 11, 1856. The first graduating class of 4 female students in 1856 would grow to more than 216 enrolled students by 1859, with 29 graduating that same year. In 1909, the facility was moved to Montgomery after the Civil War and established itself as a major institution of higher learning. In 1934 the first male student graduated from Huntingdon College and the school's rich heritage and legacy thrives to this day.

Strolling along the grounds of this small campus, you can admire some of the south's finest architecture. The richly ornate and inviting buildings such as Flowers Hall, built in 1909, are regal in appearance, to say the least. The building was designed by Herbert Langsford Warren of England, a professor of architecture from Harvard. Warren's concept was to mirror the Gothic structures of Cambridge and Oxford, and he used the Chapel of Saint James from Cambridge as a guideline for Ligon Chapel, located inside Flowers Hall. Flowers Hall is reminiscent of a Gothic cathedral, complete with stained glass, carved stone tiles in floral patterns, elaborate marble and lavish red brick, which make it a beautiful but imposing sight.

Within the corridors of Flowers Hall, in the Ligon Chapel, rumors of a phantom come up from time to time. The newly renovated facility is now used to hold many different events, including religious ceremonies,

Flowers Hall, located at Huntingdon College, shares many secrets and some legendary spirits.

concerts and weddings. Occasionally a strange robed figure is seen during those events near the extravagant pipe organ. Others have reported seeing the reflection of a shadowy figure in the splendid green stained glass in the chapel. No one really knows who or what the oddly shaped figure is or why it's there, but the majority of these sightings reported to the college staff are swept under the rug, dismissed or ignored by those who are intrigued enough to ask. It's a mystery as to why the staff closely guards the sightings of this phantom.

Other displays of fine, early American ingenuity in architecture can be found in Pratt Hall. Built in 1912 and named for Julia Pratt of Prattville, Alabama, this building may house more than just student organizations and clubs. The building was once the living quarters of the college president and his family but has been dorms for students and faculty alike over the years. Perhaps the most noted spirit of this campus and absolutely one of Alabama's most famous is the ghost of Martha, also known as the "the Red Lady." This Huntingdon legend was made famous by beloved Alabama author Kathryn Tucker Windham in her book, *13 Alabama Ghosts and Jeffery.*

The legend of the Red Lady, according to Windham, speaks of a woman named Martha, originally from New York, who had a strange obsession with the color red. Martha kept trinkets of red, red curtains and even a red bedspread. She dressed in red very often and carried a red parasol on her arrival to Huntingdon, which she attended per her father's request. She was very apprehensive about coming to Alabama since she knew no one and had no friends. She found it difficult to make friends at Huntingdon and went through several roommates before the house mother moved in with her. She, too, found Martha to be cold and isolated and moved out after only a week.

After multiple failed attempts by Martha's fellow housemates to befriend the unusual girl, many began to shun her and find excuses not to converse or even be in the same room with her. This took an exceptional toll on Martha, and she would prevail in her solitude by slashing her wrist and bleeding to death in her dormitory, located on the third floor. Today her spirit is said to wander the corridors of Pratt Hall, and on the anniversary of her death, rays of bold red light can still be seen inside her former living quarters. This legend, however, is older than Huntingdon College. The first apparition of a "Red Lady," also noted by Windham, was initially documented at the original location of Huntingdon in Tuskegee.

Pratt Hall at Huntingdon College was made famous by Alabama author Kathryn Tucker Windham in her book *13 Alabama Ghosts and Jeffrey*.

Reports from the Tuskegee Female College state that a ghostly apparition of a woman, dressed in red, walked up and down the halls all hours of the night in Sky Alley (the upper floor of the institution). This ghostly woman caused many of the female students to barricade themselves in their rooms at night while they were forced to undergo the psychological torture of listening to the clicking of her heels, up and down the hallways as they grew louder and louder until the dawn, when she would vanish into the morning light.

Today at Huntingdon College a few more spirits reside on the campus besides the infamous Red Lady. There have been reports of another ghost that makes his home in the Houghton Memorial Library. With no origin, the library ghost has no real historical representation at Huntingdon. In fact, this poor nameless specter didn't even have a name until 1990, when a student dubiously dubbed the phantom prankster "Frank," thus giving rise to "Frank the Library Ghost." Tales of haunted libraries are spread throughout history and verbal tradition. Libraries seem to be a very common location for spirits to inhabit (possibly due to the ominous scene in the 1984 film *Ghostbusters*); however, this spirit is not a grotesque and menacing entity. Frank's pranks have definitely caught more than a few unsuspecting students and faculty off guard. His antics of moving chairs, slamming doors and ghostly moaning are still scary enough to distract even the most focused student.

Eric A. Kidwell has been the library director at Houghton Memorial Library for twenty-seven years and reports that personal experiences with Frank the Library Ghost are not a new phenomenon. The director prior to his tenure knew of the ghost, as did the librarian prior to that. According to Mr. Kidwell, a former librarian who had a number of experiences with Frank was closing up the library one evening with her husband. Due to Frank's unpredictable nature, she did not like to be in the building after dark and definitely did not like to be alone. Her husband was aware of his wife's experiences with Frank and how he would frequently move her desk chair from a high sitting position to a low sitting position in her office, but he didn't think much of it.

As the couple closed up the library that evening, he noticed an open book on a table that had been left out in the study area. He went over and closed the book and took it to its designated place on the shelf. He left to join his wife, but while they were leaving, he noticed the book was again out on the table in the study. He walked over to the table and saw it was the same book he had just placed on the shelf. It was lying open to the same page it had been prior to him removing it. This more than bewildered the gentleman, and from that point on, he never discredited any more of his wife's experiences with Frank. His wife, on the other hand, had more than her fair share of Frank's shenanigans while working at Houghton Library. She frequently would become so upset with the moving of objects, falling books and moaning sounds that she would directly ask Frank to "Stop!" at which point, Frank would oblige her and indeed stop his ghostly taunting.

Mr. Kidwell also said that Frank is still involved in his ghostly antics, scaring the staff occasionally and a few students here and there. Frequently Frank is to blame for the slamming of the heavy library doors in the building. These large wooden doors weigh several hundred pounds but are often slammed and moved by a force unseen. Blaming Frank seems logical since even a strong wind wouldn't be substantial enough to budge these enormous doors. Frank has gained a fair amount of respect at Houghton as well. You can find Frank's Study directly across from the Kathryn Tucker Windham Study in the library and also Frank's chair, which rolls around the library on its own, perhaps in search of a good ghost story.

Frank's Study is located inside the Houghton Memorial Library.

Good ghost stories aren't in short supply at Huntingdon. Another spirit of a more recently deceased young man allegedly haunts the campus green. Rumors are vast regarding his demise, from a distraught student who shot himself over a break-up with his girlfriend to a sad and depressed young man failing out of school who took his own life. The circumstances may vary, but many agree that the manner of his death was suicide. Regardless of what led this poor young man to his death, he was found dead on a stage located on the campus green. Today many students using the green to lounge and study find themselves spooked to a degree of panic when this lonely spirit emerges from the afterlife. His spirit likes to take a physical approach toward his victims and will touch and grab people within his

The Houghton Memorial Library is the home of "Frank the Library Ghost" at Huntingdon College.

reach. It's also been reported that his spirit may have been responsible for an alleged episode of "possession."

One evening, some students gathered on the green and discussed the campus legends and ghost stories. In doing so, one young lady began to have some unusual sensations and felt as if she was "drifting away." Her friends noticed her awkward appearance and strange frightful calm as if the life had been drained from her very soul. She sat motionless and quiet for a few seconds, and then suddenly she spoke. However, the voice that spoke was not her own. This voice, according to her friends, spoke several words, but none made sense. Fearing at that point that their friend was in the grips of possession, they grabbed her and shook her violently until she regained composure. The voice that was not hers subsided as she regained herself. Those students still believe that their young friend was being taken over by a force they could not see.

Campus legends and ghost stories are prominent at Huntingdon College in Montgomery, Alabama. A day trip to the campus can turn up a multitude of experiences for the curious individual or paranormal enthusiast, but be advised, the spirits of Huntingdon are many and, depending on who you ask, could be many, many more.

THE LADY AT LUCAS TAVERN

M any historically significant buildings, homes and other residential structures from and around Montgomery have been moved into an area located downtown called the Old Alabama Town. The Old Alabama town consists of more than fifty restored and renovated homes from the nineteenth and twentieth centuries. The city of Montgomery and the Landmarks Foundation have a common interest in keeping the history of these buildings and homes alive for future generations of Alabamians to enjoy. Daily tours are given for a small fee, complete with tour guides dressed in authentic Victorian-era and pioneer clothing. Several locations, like the Orderman House, which is original to the location; the Rose House; and the Lucas Tavern, make for great historical and fact-filled field trips for schoolchildren or a weekend outing for history buffs.

The Lucas Tavern, circa 1818, was originally located a few miles outside of the Montgomery city limits near Waugh, a few hundred feet west of where the Creek Indian Territory began on the (then) federal road. Today, this area separates Macon and Montgomery Counties in Alabama. The tavern's original owner was James Abercrombie. In January 1821, Walter Ballard Lucas gained control of it and began to run it with the help of his second wife, Eliza Lucas Butts. Walter Lucas ran a successful cotton gin and mercantile business and bought much of the county's cotton and traded with local Indians. Eliza ran the tavern and prided herself in the hospitable atmosphere she provided her overnight customers and travelers.

From 1820 until 1840, the Lucas Tavern was considered one of the most upscale inns in the native territories. Many considerable comforts were available to guests, including the four bedrooms, which offered clean and spacious lodging; a dining area; a kitchen; and a tavern. The menu consisted of wild game like chicken, ham and venison; garden-grown vegetables; breads; pudding desserts; preserved fruit; and even brandy and wine. Eliza's meticulous attention to the comforts of her guests made her an exceptional host, and many people stayed at the tavern to enjoy the hospitality. In the spring of 1825, Revolutionary general Gilbert du Motier, Marquis de Lafayette stayed at the tavern while touring the Indian territories. Lafayette was a French-born aristocrat and military officer who served in the French Revolution and under General George Washington in the American Revolution.

In 1840, the tavern was sold and became a private residence for more than one hundred years. It was abandoned and deteriorating by the 1960s before the Landmarks Foundation rescued it in 1978. The organization moved it to the Old Alabama Town and started restoration, which was complete by 1980. The four bedrooms in the tavern became the offices of the visitors' center staff, and other parts of the building were restored to their original functions, complete with period furniture and furnishings.

It wasn't long after the restorations were complete that stories of a ghostly apparition started to circulate among the staff and visitors. Frequently, the ghost of a five-foot, petite woman dressed in nineteenth-century clothing is seen in the front doorway of the Lucas Tavern. Though some dismiss their first sighting as one of the tour guides, many report that on entering the tavern, they are informed that none of the tour guides are dressed to their description or that no female guides are on duty. If that's not suspicious enough, other stories of this apparition are common regarding her hospitable nature and pleasant demeanor when approached, leading many to believe she is indeed the ghost of Eliza Lucas.

In the mid-1980s, several stories were documented in accordance with the ghostly behavior of Eliza. One summer afternoon, a photographer ventured to the Lucas Tavern in Old Alabama Town to photograph the tavern and the schoolhouse located just behind it. He set up his equipment in the schoolhouse and admired the furnishings, complete with wooden desks, writing slates, teacher's desk and blackboard. He didn't see her at first, but a young woman, whom he presumed was an actor or guide, was sitting pleasantly enjoying a book. He ceased the opportunity to photograph

The ghost of a five-foot, petite woman dressed in nineteenth-century clothing is seen in the front doorway of the Lucas Tavern. Many believe this is the spirit of Eliza Lucas.

her and took several pictures while she paid no attention to him at all. He moved in a bit closer and, in doing so, kicked the tripod of his camera. He let out a shout, and the woman suddenly became aware of his presence. She bolted for the door, but the photographer pleaded with her to stay for a few more photos. He didn't notice until moments later that she appeared to be hovering just slightly above the floor before turning into the wall and vanishing into it.

Another story was acknowledged by the visitors' center staff while hosting a meeting at the tavern regarding restoration changes that were to take place in some of the buildings, including the Lucas Tavern. One gentleman became somewhat annoyed by the conversation and was very belligerent in his ranting regarding the impending projects. While he was voicing his opinion so angrily, the fireplace just near him let out a loud belch, and a hazy plume of ashes and soot spread out across the floor several feet in diameter, covering the angry man from head to toe in the dust. Those who believe in Eliza think that she caused the fireplace to spit out the soot to teach the angry man a valuable lesson in manners and possibly to show that she is still very much a part of the tavern.

An Old Alabama Town staff member, who anonymously contributed to this story, also gave an account of a personal experience that took place at the Lucas Tavern. One winter afternoon, the OAT member saw a woman dressed in period clothing who he presumed at the time was a fellow worker. He did not take into consideration the legend of Eliza Lucas but told another staff member about the experience. Later that day, as he broke for lunch, he was sitting in one of the rooms of the tavern and decided to make a phone call. He was on the phone when he heard the door squeak open. As he looked up in mid-conversation, the door suddenly slammed itself shut with a loud bang. He was so frightened by the experience that he shouted loudly while on the phone, giving the other caller a shock as well.

Today the tavern is still in working order as the visitors' center and is, in fact, the oldest remaining building in Montgomery County. Guided tours will inform you of the history of the Lucas Tavern, as will the Haunted Hearse Tours of Montgomery. Occasionally, people passing by the tavern at night still get a glimpse of Eliza in their photos and with the naked eye. Her spirit is still very much alive inside her old establishment and lets everyone know that she intends to continue her work in keeping her guests comfortable and satisfied, keeping tabs on her visitors even from beyond the grave.

SPIRITS OF THE
STATE CAPITOL BUILDING

Montgomery, Alabama, was not the first location selected to hold the prestigious and grand title of capital. In fact, four other locations in Alabama have held the title at one point or another. In 1817, Saint Stephens, located in Washington County, was declared the first territorial capital. In 1819, it was moved to Huntsville, located in North Alabama, and in 1820, the first "permanent" capital was moved to Cahaba. Just six years later, in 1826, the capital moved again to Tuscaloosa, Alabama, and finally in 1846 was moved into its official and permanent location in Montgomery, Alabama.

The land where the capitol building is located belonged to Andrew Dexter, one of the founding fathers of Montgomery. Mr. Dexter owned several hundred acres in the early years of Montgomery and had anticipated that this particular piece of his property would be used for the state capitol's construction. Because the property was formerly used as a pasture for livestock, the location still carries with it the ancient nickname of "Goat Hill."

The state capitol building was designed by Stephen Decatur Button in a traditional Greek-revival style with some influences of French and European neoclassical architecture. Construction started in 1846, and the building was dedicated to the city of Montgomery on December 6, 1847. On December 14, 1849, the building was destroyed by a catastrophic fire, but by March 1850, the rubble and debris from the fire were cleared and construction started on the current building, located several blocks from the original location, which was near the Court Square fountain. In October 1851, the new building was occupied by the Alabama legislature for the first time. Its permanent location now serves as the official office of the governor and is a historic landmark.

Inside the state capitol, you will find many interesting and historical treasures, preserved here for tourists, historians, enthusiasts and schoolchildren all venturing to the capitol for a little history lesson on Montgomery and the state of Alabama. From February to May 1861, the state capitol building served as the first White House of the Confederacy. A large bronze star located in the interior of the front portico marks the exact spot where Jefferson Davis stood when he took the oath of office on February 18, 1861. Other features on the grounds outside the building include the Confederate Memorial monument, dedicated to over one hundred thousand Civil War veterans for their patriotism, and the Avenue of Flags that can be found on the southern lawn. This pathway features a flag representing each state in the United States with an engraved stone at the base of each one.

The state capitol building has a lot of history and many sights to take in, but least known to the tourists and visitors are the ghost stories associated with the state capitol building. According to who you talk to, the ghost stories from the state capitol building tend to vary, from how many spirits haunt the capitol building to how ghostly in nature they are. According to local legend and more than a few of the city's historians, at least three spirits are most commonly referred to as the "spirit of the state capitol building."

One of these rumored spirits is that of a beautiful blonde woman. Nameless and faceless, she roams the halls of the building in search of what many believe to be her soldier returning from the War Between the States. Typically she is referred to as the "Confederate widow" but not just because of the story of her Confederate beau. Those who have seen this strange woman roaming the halls of the capitol building at night say that her dress and attire matches that of the antebellum era. Few say they have actually seen her face, but nearly every report includes the blonde ringlets that can be seen hanging harmoniously under her grey bonnet. Often people report hearing the rustling sound of her dress as she passes up and down the halls; it's a most unnerving sound to some who work in the building in the late hours.

Though sanitation employees working late inside the building most often report the unnatural sound of the Confederate widow's rustling dress, she is occasionally spotted inside the top of the dome at night. Upon entering the second-floor rotunda, the dome can be accessed by just a few hundred stairs or so. At the highest point of the dome, a small room is lit day and night. Most often it's the passerby who gets a glance at her staring down from high above the capitol in the evening, her head hung low as if in mourning.

Other ghosts who haunt the capitol are a bit more historical and their stories a bit more frightening. On Halloween night 1912, a murder took place in the capitol building. Sources of this murder are limited, but a lone article from the *Montgomery Advertiser* titled "Will Oakley Kills Step-Father, P.A. Woods, at Capitol: Dead Man Is Shot Four Times with 41 Caliber Revolver—Slayer Offers Him Pistol For A Duel" reveals the gruesome and terrifying circumstances that led to this murder.

In 1912, a property suit was filed regarding the division of family land owned by P.A. Woods of Odenville, Alabama. His stepson, Will Oakley, was eighteen years old and a farmer from St. Clair County. The feud over the property division had been going on for some time, and the Thursday prior to the murder, Mr. Woods, Will and his half uncle J.G. Oakley (who was president of the convict board) met at the State Capitol Building in the office of the state convict board to give disposition on the case. Will had been wearing a pistol in a shoulder harness all day. It was visible and, for the most part, in plain sight. This was disturbing to see since Will was a noted hothead who feared little. He had made the statement at one point during the disposition that he had been in the army and wasn't afraid of anyone.

After the conclusion of the disposition, just before three o'clock that afternoon, Will became enraged when the outcome of the case didn't turn out in his favor, and he began threatening his stepfather. He warned him that he'd better not leave the building without a bodyguard. J.G. was uneasy at the behavior of his nephew and feared that he may just be crazy enough to kill someone. It wasn't long before his fears would manifest into reality. Will and his stepfather were opposite each other over the desk when Will produced two pistols from his coat and offered his stepfather one in a duel. P.A. Woods pleaded with Will not to kill him. J.G. feared for his life and that of his brother-in-law and quickly left the room to seek aid in the matter. Seconds later, four shots rang out from the office, and Will Oakley fled the room and down the stairs of the capitol building.

Will made a steady and hasty retreat from the building, down Washington Street, and headed to the county jail to turn himself in. He was followed by a black man who heard the shots and saw him fleeing the building. He was apprehended by the sheriff just before making his way inside the jail. Will was immediately arrested and searched. Two, 41-caliber pistols and a knife were taken from him. Will also refused an attorney and said, "I shot a man, and I was justified in doing so." He refused any further statements and was charged with murder the following day. The coroner's report stated that the fatal shot that killed P.A. Woods most likely came from the first shot to his neck, which

On Halloween night 1912, a murder took place in the Montgomery capitol building. The killer's spirit returns to wash the blood from his hands.

pierced his jugular. The three remaining gunshots were all in the abdomen, which implies they came after the victim was already on the ground. This was also confirmed by the powder burns found on the face and neck of P.A. Woods.

Will Oakley was inevitably sent to prison, and over the years, the excitement from the shooting has subsided greatly. Most people have never heard the story of P.A. Woods and Will Oakley, but a strange and unusual phenomenon associated with the murder is still happening in the capitol building today. Since the murder, employees and state officials who worked in the offices of the state convict board have noticed that they would often find the water mysteriously running in the bathroom sinks. Even after years of renovations and makeovers to the building, the water continues to run from the faucets.

Legend says it's the ghost of Will Oakley, returning to the scene of the crime to wash the blood from his hands. Will's anger and anxious personality may have condemned him in the afterlife, or he may have some unfinished business to take care of. Or is it that his soul cannot rest until he has made amends for the dreadful deed he committed? That's a question only he can answer. Still, it's doubtful anyone living or dead would want to approach him to ask. If he's still washing one hundred years of blood from his hands, he may have more to make amends for.

THE OLD HILL INFIRMARY

The structure and function of the human heart is designed to pump blood through the vascular system in the human body. Mazes of tangled veins and arteries work as a connecting system carrying oxygen-rich blood to organs, muscles and tissue. Connections to the nervous system intertwine the brain as the central hub of communication where thought and emotion provoke reactions throughout the entire body. The idea that the heart holds emotional ties is more theorized in cultural beliefs than proven by modern medicine. Still, all these aspects pertain to a story about a young boy who was saved by medicine and of the women who were tortured by it. This is the story of Henry Myrick, who grew to adulthood in life, only to come back as the spirit of a thirteen-year-old boy. He is locked together in legend with the pleading souls of three women from a former hospital on South Perry Street.

In 1897, Doctor Luther Leonidas Hill and his brother, Robert, established the Laura Hill Hospital in Montgomery, Alabama. Luther Leonidas Hill was born in Montgomery on January 22, 1862. He initially started his education in ministry to follow in the footsteps of his father, Reverend Luther Hill. However, in 1878, he changed his direction in education and began his studies in medicine at Howard College (now Samford University) in Birmingham, Alabama. He continued his education and graduated with a medical degree in 1881 from City University in New York.

In 1882, he dedicated more of his education to medical study at Jefferson College in Philadelphia, Pennsylvania, where he incorporated surgical procedures for eye, ear and throat surgeries. In July 1883, Dr. Hill went to London, England, where he became a student of Joseph Lister, a leading pioneer in the field of sterile surgical procedures. He studied with Lister as his mentor for several years until he returned to Montgomery and opened his own private practice, known as the Hill Infirmary (later called the Laura Hill Hospital). In 1888, Dr. Hill married Lillie Lyons from Mobile, Alabama. They had five children, one of whom grew up to become an Alabama senator. This son, Lister Hill, was named for Dr. Hill's mentor from England.

After he established the Hill Infirmary on South Perry Street, he published an article in the *New York Medical Record* in 1900 called "Wounds of the Heart." Hill's extensive knowledge in vascular medicine made him a leading authority in medical procedures involving the heart, and doctors and medical students alike looked to him for his expertise in the leading surgical methods of that time. Though Dr. Hill had treated patients for different afflictions and ailments, he had never worked on a living heart until one September afternoon when a young man named Henry Myrick would cause Dr. Hill to change medical history in the Western hemisphere.

Henry Myrick was a thirteen-year-old African American boy who lived in Montgomery. He was stabbed in the heart, and though how and why he was stabbed is perhaps lost to history, the condition of the wound is well documented. For more than six hours, Henry bled from his stab wound located in the left ventricle. Two doctors were called to help him, but both agreed that they could not treat the boy. Finally, Dr. Hill was summoned, and though Henry's family was reluctant, Dr. Hill convinced them to allow him to operate in an attempt to save Henry's life.

Dr. Hill had to wait until another doctor arrived to administer chloroform to the boy before he could operate, and with the help of his brother Robert and a fourth doctor attending him, they moved Henry to a table in his office and performed the surgery by lantern light. Dr. Hill was an expert, but he was nervous. This was the first living heart he had ever operated on. He set up for surgery and opened the boy's chest. He saw that Henry's chest cavity was filled with blood, indicating there was massive internal bleeding from the wound. He opened the pericardial sack (the thin lining of tissue located around the heart) to alleviate the pressure and allow the blood to drain. He then carefully stitched up the left ventricle with a catgut suture. A catgut suture, contrary to the belief, is not made of feline intestines. It comes from the term used in primitive medicine referring to "cattlegut" stitches or sutures. The intestines of animals like cattle, goats and sheep have been used for medicinal purposes for thousands of years.

With the closing the wound, the entire procedure took about forty-five minutes, and Henry made a complete recovery in just a few weeks. This

The Old Hill Infirmary is rumored to be haunted by more than one spirit.

was the event in Dr. Hill's career that would send him into the history books regarding medical procedures and vascular medicine. It was the first successful attempt to repair a wound in the heart, and Henry was grateful that Dr. Hill had saved his life. Later in adulthood, Henry moved to Detroit, Michigan, where he was involved in a fight. The altercation quickly went bad when one of the men involved pulled a knife and stabbed Henry in the heart. Whether this incident was caused by curse or convenience, Henry did not survive this injury to his heart and died shortly after.

Rumors and stories came out many years later about the strange activity that took place in the old hospital building. Stories were whispered about a ghostly young man that wanders the building at night, the haunting figure of a woman in white and strange voices that sounded like a woman pleading for her life. Often things would move with no one around and be misplaced.

Today, rumors of the ghostly antics are more common than paranormal events, but the story of Henry Myrick is a vaguely known part of the frightful fabric woven into Montgomery's haunted history.

What is known about the former hospital building is that at least one apparition is most likely Henry Myrick; though murdered in adulthood, the young Henry seeks out Dr. Hill to save him once again. Others are less known and even more mysterious. The strange lady in white whose voice is heard pleading and begging is speculated to have been a patient of another doctor who used the facility before Dr. Hill. However, this doctor was not so pleasant.

Dr. James Marion Sims was a pioneering doctor in woman's medicine and is also known as the father of modern gynecology. He was born in South Carolina and received his medical education at South Carolina College in Columbia. He studied under Dr. Churchill Jones in Lancaster, South Carolina, and was required to take a short, three-month course in Charleston before he moved to Philadelphia, Pennsylvania, where he was enrolled in Jefferson Medical College and graduated in 1835. He promptly moved back to Lancaster to practice, but after the suspicious deaths of two of his patients, he moved to Alabama, where he continued his work in women's health. He would later travel back to Lancaster to marry Theresa Jones, the daughter of a prominent physician. Dr. Sims and his wife then moved back to Alabama and opened a women's hospital on South Perry Street.

It wasn't long before Dr. Sims would be under suspicion again. According to reports, Dr. Sims held three African American slave women captive and conducted numerous experiments on them. Various invasive procedures were conducted without anesthesia, resulting in painful and agonizing torture. The three women, only known as Anarcha, Betsy and Lucy, suffered terrible experimental surgeries from 1845 until 1849, in an effort to repair a condition called vesicovaginal fistulas. This condition is typically the result of prolonged and traumatic labor. Pressure from childbirth causes a restriction in blood flow to the vesicovaginal wall, causing tissue to die and leave a hole that allows urine from the bladder to leak into the vaginal canal. Dr. Sims perfected his procedure for vesicovaginal fistulas on Anarcha after more than thirty surgeries, and later it was successfully administered under anesthesia to a white woman.

Dr. Sims's peculiar experiments didn't just stop there. He also experimented on the infants and children of slave women as well. His vile and cruel methods of treating trismus, a condition that causes the jaw to swell, locking the mouth in a tight closed position, were inhuman and completely unorthodox, even by primitive standards of medicine. It was noted that he used an awl (a spiked metal tool used to puncture hard leather by shoemakers) to unhinge to jaws of these children in an effort to find a cause for the condition. Driven by experimental medical science of the day and with no logical explanation for his perverse behavior, Dr. Sims eventually moved out of Alabama after much controversy over his methods and experimental procedures. He eventually found his way to France and England during the Civil War. There he again experimented with gynecological procedures in an effort to control hysteria in woman whose husbands and fathers could not commit them to psychiatric hospitals for treatment, treating them instead, on an outpatient basis. In 1871, Dr. Sims returned to the States and lived in New York, where he advocated having cancer patients admitted to the women's hospital there. Speculation was heavy that this was a ploy to gain more patients for experimental procedures. Sims planned a return trip to Europe to advance his work when he died of a sudden heart attack on November 13, 1883.

Today the horror stories of his grotesque experiments ring a haunting and familiar chime, bringing to mind the terrible and notoriously haunted LaLaurie Mansion in New Orleans, Louisiana, where in 1834, a similar situation unfolded. After the death of a young slave girl and a tragic fire, police investigated the LaLaurie family. They uncovered a sinister sight and found slaves bound and kept in cages, walled up like animals and abused in the worst ways. They had also been experimented on and kept in horrendous conditions.

These cruel and similar circumstances may be what has trapped the spirits of the Old Hill Infirmary in a purgatory of tragedy. The ghostly voices at the old hospital on South Perry Street can still be heard on occasion, pleading in conversations. Is it Anarcha, Betsy or possibly Lucy that frantically pleads with Henry to hide him from the doctor? Is she afraid of what terrible torture she will have to endure next in the name of medicine? It's uncertain, as with all supernatural experiences. However, given the history of the old building on South Perry Street, if you're looking for a doctor, don't stop here: it's possible you'd be better off dead.

A Temporary Home
for Eternal Spirits

As stories of spirits and ghosts come and go throughout history, many historical locations have some form of legend or myth. Some are true and live on for generation after generation. Others come and go with time and occasionally are forgotten and erased altogether. Depending on the person or location, some legends can be more believable than others, and depending on whom you ask, some prefer the stories of ghosts and ghostly activity be forgotten altogether. It's understandable that some people who choose to forget certain aspects of the paranormal, as it pertains to history, are justified in doing so. Sometimes, stories of ghosts scare people away; others are attracted to them and seek out the unusual history of how the ghost story came to be. These circumstances are true for one location in Montgomery, Alabama, and are debated by staff and visitors alike, but what happens when skeptical visitors come for history and leave with a haunting experience they remember for a lifetime?

Just adjacent to the capitol building, located at 644 Washington Avenue, you will find a quaint and stately home. The original location of the home was at 301 Bibb Street (now a skate park). It was moved from that location some ten blocks away to its current location. It was built in 1830 and originally was the home to Joseph Samuel Prince Winter. Today, this quiet manor is known as the "First White House of the Confederacy" and was a former residence of Confederate president Jefferson Davis and his family from February until May 1861.

Though they only spent a few months living here, some of the Davis family's personal belongings are on display in this now renovated museum. Personal effects of Jefferson Davis himself include military-issued items and his personal journal correspondence kept during the Civil War. Other items featured in the home belonged to his family. Varina Davis's clothing and personal items, like hair combs and accessories, are also here. Most of the home's furnishings are reproduced but are appropriate for the antebellum era. The actual furnishings belonging to the Davis family were moved to Virginia after the capital of the Confederacy was moved to Richmond in May 1861.

Visitors and history buffs from all over the world visit the First White House of the Confederacy yearly, and on occasion, visitors leave with more than a spooky reminder of the home's short history. Though staff and tour guides at the house will shy away from questions concerning ghosts and supernatural goings-on, it doesn't keep the public from talking about things that go bump at the museum. While looking for interviews for this story, I was reminded of how difficult it is for people to talk about paranormal experiences. However, it didn't stop a handful of patrons from talking about their own experiences while visiting.

During a daily tour of the First White House of the Confederacy, a local woman and her husband spent the better part of about three hours touring the home and taking in all the historical information. Though she asked to remain anonymous for this interview, she did permit me to say that she is an eighth-grade history teacher, which is essentially what provoked her to visit the museum. "It was early spring, May the seventh, to be exact," she said, "and I was looking for material for a possible field trip with my students before school ended. I was looking over the artifacts encased in the upstairs room and noticed the sound of rustling curtains. I felt like I would have seen or heard another person come in the room, but I hadn't noticed anyone, so I just went on looking over the artifacts."

After regrouping with her husband and making her way downstairs to leave, she told a staff member that there was an odd draft upstairs and that a window may be open, causing the curtains to blow. The staff member replied by telling her the windows do not open, and it would be impossible for that to happen. The anonymous schoolteacher didn't make much of an effort to respond since her husband was rushing her out the door, but on the way out, as she passed the house on the sidewalk, she looked up at the window in the room where she had heard the rustling sound and saw a dark-haired woman standing at the window. The woman in the window was wearing a pale-colored pastel dress with fancy gloves. When she stopped on the sidewalk to stare at the woman in the window, they made eye contact, and the strange woman quickly vanished from the schoolteacher's sight. "I wasn't frightened or scared," she said. "But it did make me wonder if I had seen a ghost. I have had other experiences similar to this one, but she didn't seem real; it was like she had not intended to be seen at all."

The schoolteacher never followed up with the staff at the First White House of the Confederacy to find out whether any of the museum's employees or volunteers could have been dressed like the woman she saw. But conveniently, the very same week, another report came from a different visitor who had also been to the museum and had a similar experience. This patron was also upstairs and saw the same woman in a pastel dress with white gloves walk down the staircase. She followed her downstairs and lost track of her as she passed into the back of the hallway and into the downstairs parlor. Oddly, when the woman followed her path, she noticed that a rope prohibited her from crossing over into the parlor. She was a bit concerned and asked the staff about what she had seen. It was confirmed at that point that no reenactors were on hand at the museum and none of the staff was dressed to fit the description she gave.

The First White House of the Confederacy was home to Jefferson Davis and his family from February until May of 1861.

Confused and a little annoyed, the patron left but wondered if she had seen a spirit that day as well. It's possible some lingering spirit has taken up residence in the First White House of the Confederacy. It is unknown as to whether this ghostly woman in pastel is a member of the Davis family or perhaps just some random specter who is wandering through a vortex or rift in time. The description has left some to speculate that she is a member of the Davis family. The ghostly woman bears a striking likeness to the painting in the downstairs living room. Again, it's only speculation that these reports are indeed paranormal. However, the staff at the First White House of the Confederacy will not acknowledge them as much more than nonsense, but on occasion, you do hear a rumor or two about the staff's personal experiences.

It's likely they are hiding something very supernatural or maybe protecting their resident ghost from the prying eyes of ghost hunters and thrill seekers. As with the Davis family, who moved from Montgomery to Richmond when the war engaged in hostilities, she may be waiting for the return of her family or perhaps the end of the war. Still, a presence can be felt inside the home on Washington Avenue—felt but not heard or seen, except to a select few.

HAUNTED DORMS AT
MAXWELL AIR FORCE BASE

In December 1903, two brothers from Kitty Hawk, North Carolina, Orville and Wilbur Wright, developed the first successful fixed-wing aircraft flown by man. They became successful in the development of machine controls and aviation engineering and are known today throughout the world as the founding fathers of modern aviation. They were contracted through the United States Army to build planes and teach pilots how to fly. They also established a civilian flying school in 1910, in Montgomery, Alabama, near the Maxwell Air Force Base and Gunter Annex. By 1920, Montgomery was a central hub for aerial mail. In 1930, the Army Air Corps Tactical School moved to Maxwell and had established itself as a major university for air military training by 1946.

Today, the base is still functional and is home to more than twelve thousand active duty, reserve, contracted and civilian personnel. The facility is regarded as a major contributor to flight education as well as space and cyberspace-powered engineering. The Maxwell Air Force base is located just a few miles outside of the downtown district in Montgomery, and gaining access to the base without the proper consent is nearly impossible. It may be difficult to gain civilian access to this location, but for the spirits that haunt the base, authority and permission is not a necessity.

After 1910, during the time the location was an established flight school, many experimental projects and faulty engineering caused a number of crashes that killed an undisclosed amount of people. Primitive engineering was unsafe, and taking a plane ride in the early days of aviation and engineering was not only dangerous, it was also downright disastrous.

The hauntings at the base have been around for a long time. Some say the spirits that haunt building 1433 are those lost in the many crashes that took place at the flight school. Others dismiss the stories as tall tales. Some students and air force personnel staying in the dormitories in building 1433 have reported a number of unusual circumstances that take the form of a physical manifestation. Nightmares have been the most common trend among the students here. Dreams of horrible plane crashes and fires are certainly scary, but waking up to a room that is filled with smoke has also been reported, and that would terrify anyone, with or without military training.

Other unusual happenings take place when students on the second floor wake up to the smell of burning electrics, and appliances are rendered useless either by frequently shorting out or going completely haywire. Some have seen what they describe as ghost soldiers near the Alabama River, located just a few hundred yards from the facility. Although it's speculated that these soldier-like apparitions are possibly Confederate soldiers who drowned crossing the river during the Civil War, it's also a common rumor that the spirits associated with those apparitions do not like students with northern or foreign accents. They are most often the target of these spirits, and it's those students who report seeing them the most.

There has been at least one documented sighting of something supernatural at Maxwell Air Force Base. A civil engineer named Tom Rucker said he knew someone who lived in the base housing near the library years ago. Rucker reported a photo taken by a friend of his children in their living room that revealed a strange anomaly behind them. It is unclear as to what the image actually was, but Rucker did note that it did not appear to be a double exposure or faulty function of the camera.

Roaming spirits of dead Union and Confederate soldiers could reside on the base since it is a military installation, or perhaps those who lost their lives here in fiery crashes have somehow become part of the natural landscape. Stories about ghosts at Maxwell's haunted dorms aren't going away, even with the secretive nature of the military. Paranormal researchers and investigators have been trying for years to gain access to the base to conduct investigations and are very familiar with the reports of activity. It's become part of the history of the base to a degree. Those experiencing the phenomenon will keep the stories circulating as long as the ghosts reside there. Knowing is half the battle, and the acknowledgment of these spectral wonders may be all these spirits need to finally rest in peace, but until that happens, just like the aviation school students, these spirits will take flight.

CAPITOL PLAZA

TOWER OF TERROR

W hat happens to a home or location when tragedy strikes? Does the impact of a traumatic event embed itself into the foundations? What kind of supernatural occurrence causes one to suffer the ghosts of those who perished under tragic circumstances? Is there a way to cleanse the stigma of an awful event from a location? These are all questions many people may ask themselves after hearing about the ghosts that came about from a tragedy that took place at Capitol Plaza one very cold February night in 1967.

The Capitol Towers apartment building is located at 7 Clanton Street in Montgomery, Alabama. It was previously Capitol Plaza and was also known as the Walter Bragg Smith building. Dale's Penthouse Restaurant was located on the rooftop of the building. It was a posh and upscale restaurant that served many of the city's top officials and politicians.

On February 7, 1967, Ed Pepper, a widely known state politician and his wife, Ann, along with several guests who were attending a dinner party hosted at Dale's Penthouse Restaurant, spent the evening dining and discussing business relations and politics. The view from the restaurant was magnificent: a 360-degree view through the glass walls that encased this rooftop restaurant made the entire city of Montgomery viewable. Though the atmosphere was lively and fun, no one could anticipate the events that were about to unfold.

Jesse Williams, a twenty-two-year-old cook, was working that Tuesday night in the kitchen. He noticed that a small fire had broken out in the cloakroom, apparently caused by a cigarette or pipe left in a jacket pocket. Another employee was trying to put the fire out when Jesse realized he should grab the extinguisher and help the gentleman. In the few minutes it took Jesse to return with the fire extinguisher, the fire had already spread and was dangerously out of hand.

Jesse urged guests at the restaurant to take the elevator downstairs, essentially leading about twenty-six people to safety, but the rooftop restaurant was completely engulfed in flames. By the time emergency services were dispatched and reached the building, Fire Captain William McCord realized there was a serious problem. The ladders on the trucks were not long enough to reach the top of the building. According to records of that evening's events, the temperature outside was twenty-eight degrees, and the water from the fire truck was literally freezing before it could get to the blazing inferno on the top floor. This was no doubt a tragedy in itself, and the former captain stated that it was a night he would never forget. Roughly seventy-five to one hundred guests were at Dale's Penthouse that night, and many never made it to safety.

The fire was eventually extinguished, and firemen worked diligently around the clock to recover bodies. The lives of twenty-six people were lost, mostly staff from the restaurant. Among the dead were Ed Pepper, his wife and Sydney Zagri, a lobbyist from Washington, D.C. A few people escaped the blaze by taking the fire escape and breaking through windows to reach other exits. But the death toll would rise gradually as media and family flocked to the scene. Captain McCord recalled having to search through the rubble to find the bodies. Most were so badly burned that identifying them properly was nearly impossible. There were even a few who had huddled together, trying to shield themselves from the blaze. People from all over Montgomery came to the scene of the tragedy in the hopes that their loved ones were not among the victims. Reporters spent hours on site, lingering until dawn the following morning waiting on details and numbers concerning the casualties. Among those reporters was Rex Thomas, who recalled hearing a fireman say, "I don't think I can go up there again. I will never forget it."

As fate would have it, the massive blaze was confined to the roof, and minimal damage was inflicted on the remaining apartments in the building. The building was evacuated successfully during the fire, and only a few light fixtures burned due to the heat on the lower floors. The fire at Dale's Penthouse sparked a lot of controversy over fire safety in the city and eventually led to stricter fire codes. Though reinforcements

On February 7, 1967, a catastrophic fire destroyed Dale's Penthouse Restaurant, which was once located on the rooftop of the Capitol Towers apartment complex.

were made and renovations took place quickly, reports of ghostly activity have been reported here over the years.

As with most locations associated with paranormal phenomenon, renovations or tragedy seem to ramp up activity or inflict it on the location. In the case of the Capitol Towers apartment building, both seem to apply. The activity level of the supernatural here brings a multitude of unusual reports. People who have lived at the location over the years have seen the ghostly manifestations of figures around the upper floors and what used to be Dale's Penthouse. Mostly in the form of dark and black shadowy mists, perhaps the essence of those formerly lost at the building. The spirits cannot pass on and seem to be stuck in the realm of the living. Unfortunately, the spirits of Capitol Towers don't understand that they are not supposed to be here and pay no attention to the people still living in the building.

Most often, the shadowy apparitions witnessed by so many linger and don't cause any physical harm to those who witness them, but the sheer terror of seeing these spirits is enough to shake the most skeptical of nonbelievers. The dark figures manifest without warning and typically venture through walls or around corners and vanish almost instantly. People who live or have lived at Capitol Towers have also reported hearing screams, most likely from those trapped in the building the night of the fire. Often the shrieks of a woman are accompanied with other voices screaming, "Help me! Help us!" and it has driven a few tenants to leave the building and even move out altogether.

It's hard to understand why the dead can become trapped in a location. Or why they stay around to endure countless decades of endless wandering. Perhaps it's because the spirits of those who died in the fire of 1967 have somehow become trapped by death itself. Ancient cultures believed that fire was cleansing and by purifying a soul by burning the body, the soul would be released into the heavens. Cultures all over the world still believe in the concept of burial by fire. The tragic fire at Capitol Towers wasn't a deliberate funeral fire but damnation nonetheless.

THE WINTER PLACE

Among the beautiful remaining plantations and turn-of-the-century homes in Montgomery, Alabama, the Winter Place is perhaps one of the most curious and magnificent when referring to "haunted" houses. Long before its now dilapidated state, it was the grand and lavish home of one of Montgomery's most prominent families. Built in 1855, the Italianate-style mansion was home to Joseph Winter and his family. In the 1870s, the south house was constructed for Joseph's daughter, Sally Thorington, and her husband, Robert. The north and south buildings are connected by a long hallway and underground corridors. Three stories, including a subterranean basement, in the south house make it a wonder of underground mazes, now visible to the visitor without entering the home.

Another unusual feature of the home is the square turret on the third floor, resembling the home of Norman Bates from the 1960 Alfred Hitchcock horror film, *Psycho*. The outer décor is embellished with large, black wooden shutters that, no doubt, hide the ghastly inhabitants of this typical haunted house. The appealing and haunting beauty of the structure is, at least, a stunning encompassment of the era's architecture. It's clearly a place where a number of ghastly tales could be derived just by pure imagination, and there is no shortage of preexisting ghost stories that further establish the macabre legends of this deteriorating home. Some ghost stories of specters dressed in period clothing, peering down on the occasional visitor brave enough to glance over at the rotting structure, are common, and a few people even believe the spirits who still live here are members of the Winter family.

The Winter Place is perhaps one of the most curious and magnificent "haunted houses" in Montgomery, Alabama.

Joseph Winter was a successful businessman, and his son later became recognized as one of Montgomery's most respected judges. Though the home stayed in the family for many years, it eventually was sold after the remaining descendants died and was converted into apartments during the early 1960s and '70s. Some of the earliest supernatural tales from this estate speak of a soldier who was allegedly buried in the wall of the downstairs corridors. On occasion, General Jefferson Davis stayed at the Winter place, and at another point it was used as a meeting place for Confederate officers during the Civil War. The soldier's spirit is rumored to call out from the dusty caverns of the damp and moldy basement, peering out at those who may cross over his alleged resting place within the wall. Others have seen the uniformed soldier on the house grounds wearing what appears to be a blue uniform, leaving some to speculate that he may have been a Yankee spy and was murdered and buried within the basement walls.

Others who lived in the apartments during the 1960s reported that the spirit of a woman was frequently seen in the living quarters of the home. Believed to be the spirit of a distant relative, Winter Thorington (a direct descendant of the Thorington family) reported that the ghostly woman was none other than his aunt who haunted the apartments. Her spirit has

The apparition of a soldier, rumored to be a Yankee spy, is most often seen wandering the basement corridors of the old Winter Place.

been reported by many of the tenants who lived at the Winter Place, slowly wandering the long and elaborate hallways of the upper floors. Her face is typically drawn up in a state of confusion, as if she is looking for something. No doubt something of great importance, for whatever it is she seeks in death, she is more than determined to find it.

The peering spirit of the upper floor is typically a man. Bearded and aged, he looks onto the grounds as if watching or perhaps waiting for someone or something to show up. His white beard and full head of gray hair gives him a regal but thoughtful look. His associations with the Winter Place are fewer and far between, but his appearance is still an often sad and somber one. It's been suggested that he is mourning the death of his wife, who perhaps was one of the many who perished from the yellow fever epidemic of the late 1800s. The haunted history regarding the Winter Place is established and it harbors the spirits of the restless dead. But much like the house itself, the history and the spirits here have been abandoned and forgotten by time and by communication, nearly cut off from its once lively and bustling atmosphere. The home sits a dying effigy of the ghosts within its forgotten and dark halls.

THE WINTER BUILDING

Located in downtown Montgomery, in Court Square, just across the street from the Court Square Fountain, is the historic Winter Building. This building was built in 1841 and housed a branch of the Saint Mary's Bank. On the second floor of this building a monumental and historic event took place. On the evening of April 11, 1861, newly minted Confederate secretary of war Leroy Pope Walker, under the orders of Confederate president Jefferson Davis, sent a telegram addressed to General Pierre Gustave Toutant Beauregard at Fort Sumter in Charleston, South Carolina, that sparked the American Civil War. The Union forces at Fort Sumter occupied the military stronghold illegally, and on the morning of April 12, 1861, Confederate forces fired on the fort and fighting began.

Leroy Walker was appointed as secretary of war by Confederate president Jefferson Davis. Though Walker had no previous military training, he was chosen to take on the role because of his support for secession. He traveled to meet representatives from Tennessee to promote the cause and secession of the Confederate States of America. He was also chosen to be a Confederate representative in Europe and eventually did accept the position. President Davis made him a brigadier general in command of two garrisons in Mobile and Montgomery, Alabama, during the war, but in 1862, he resigned from his military position. He later returned to the army as a military judge in 1864.

The telegram sent from the Winter Building has a legacy, and so does Leroy Walker. The location has been used for different businesses over the years, and more than a few ghost stories and interesting tales have been told from those lucky or unlucky enough to experience them. One story comes from a former attorney's staff member who witnessed a male spirit wandering the second floor of the building. When he saw a curiously dressed man he didn't recognize as a co-worker, he followed him down the hallway. He called out to him, and the apparition turned to face him and then quickly faded away.

Coincidentally, Leroy Walker was also a well-established attorney. He's been recognized for his role as a defense attorney to legendary outlaw Frank James. Walker defended Frank James on April 25, 1884, in a trial involving the robbery of a government payroll near Muscle Shoals, Alabama. Dozens of witnesses identified Frank as the robber, but the case was heated and the cross examinations between Walker and Governor Smith were brutal. In the end, Walker was successful in his portrayal of James as a war hero, and Frank James was acquitted on all charges, walking out of the Huntsville Federal Court House (Calhoun House) in Madison County, Alabama, a free man. Leroy Walker may have reached out in spirit to this former attorney's staff member since he could identify with the legal obligations of those working in the building at the time, but his ghost is not the only one who allegedly haunts the Winter Building.

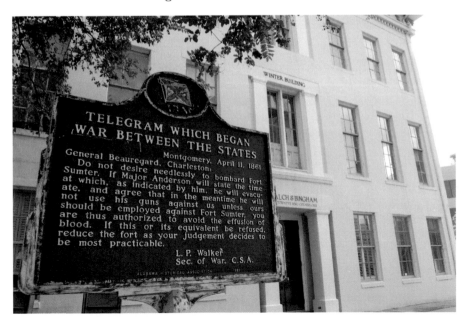

You can read about the historical significance of the Winter Building, but only tall tales embrace the forgotten tunnels beneath it.

It's established in the history of Montgomery that French explorers like Lafayette, as well as Spanish conquistadors and explorers like Tristan de Luna y Arellano, traveled through the city from trade routes established from Europe. These explorers came in search of wealth and new lands, but the trade routes were also familiar to smugglers and mercenaries who came to the shores of Montgomery by way of the Alabama River. It's rumored that underground tunnels are hiding beneath the Winter Building. Because it was built just prior to the Civil War, these alleged tunnels are most likely an extravagant tale embellished by the supernatural events that have taken place here, but some strongly believe in the stories. A few local people who anonymously contributed to this story reported that smugglers used the tunnels to bring African slaves and contraband into the city. This would have been bold indeed and a source of controversy since the former capitol building once sat on the neighboring lot, where the fountain is now located today.

A runaway slave in that time was as sought after as a horse thief or bandit. It was a crime punishable by hanging or whatever means a tracker may find necessary to remedy the problem. One Montgomery local mentioned that she had heard a story about a slave who used the tunnel as a hideout after he ran away. He hid in the tunnel for days, waiting on an opportunity to escape and follow the river north to freedom. By the time he had worked up the courage to emerge from his hiding place under the cover of night, he was met with authorities and quickly retreated back into the tunnels. Allegedly, the men in pursuit of the runaway slave were exhausted after several days of combing the riverbanks and outer counties looking for him and decided to brick him up inside the tunnel, inevitably causing his death. His tomb is forever lost and nothing more than an extravagant story now, but his spirit is rumored to be one of the few that haunts the Winter Building.

If not for outlaw attorneys, runaway slaves and a few marauding smugglers, the old building would be just as it seems today, a historical landmark awaiting a purchaser through reality. But a local distributor also mentioned a personal experience that took place while he was delivering Coke products to the location. The building's basement was used for storage when it was an attorney's office a few years ago. The gentleman who made the delivery came in to drop off several cases of drinks, but this would turn out to be no ordinary delivery. According to a second-hand report, the deliveryman was in the basement stacking the cases of drinks when he suddenly felt a cold and clammy hand touch his shoulder. He became rather anxious as he turned to see who it was and no one was there. He immediately packed up his hand truck and left without the slightest hint of a good-bye to the employees.

The building sits empty today. The historical marker in front of the Winter Building tells about the circumstances regarding the telegram that started the war. The history is what is most recognized by those who pass by the Winter Building, but forgotten is the tomb beneath it, eternally locked away in the dark and dank recesses of a hollow grave. If fate is to have its way in determining an afterlife, it seems circumstantial and maybe a bit superficial to believe that rumors and stories about one historical figure are relevant, while others go unrecognized. As for the mystery of the old building, more than a few secrets may be buried here. History tells us what is important, but occasionally, a tall tale can tell us what is forgotten.

MURDER BY FEATHER DUSTER

It was mid-July 1943. The late, humid summer hung like a damp curtain over Montgomery, Alabama. The cicadas and crickets electrified the late evening atmosphere, and a haunting cry vaguely echoed throughout the historic Garden District. The night air was as stiff as the whiskey on Mr. Holloway's breath. Kathryn stood silently still, cloaked in the still warm blood of her husband. She raised her hand and looked curiously at the item clenched in her fist.

Allegations of abuse and infidelity had begun to circulate about the Holloways in their prominent neighborhood, and rumors spread around town about Mrs. Holloway's numerous affairs. She was almost twenty years younger than her husband and very flirtatious. Being the very attractive, redheaded woman she was, she flaunted herself often, much to the dislike of her husband. Her scandals and affairs became a regular issue, but the allegations that Mr. Holloway was physically and perhaps even sexually abusive to his young wife were also part of this couples' destructive relationship. They were often seen in drunken fights, furiously arguing at their Garden District home and in different locations around town.

Two weeks prior to July 10, 1943, Mrs. Kathryn Holloway wrecked a car belonging to her husband, Dave Holloway. After a violent confrontation, Mrs. Holloway moved out of their beautiful home and into a small apartment on Alabama Street on the opposite side of town. For the past several weeks, Dave had been begging her to come back, and though she refused him at

The Garden District in Montgomery, Alabama, was the location of a horrible murder that took place in 1943.

first, eventually she gave in and agreed to meet him to sort out their martial issues.

Sometime after July 10, Kathryn came back home to settle her differences with her husband. Both had been drinking that night, and Dave made physical advances toward his wife in an effort to seduce her. She refused him, and he began to physically abuse her. Then something in her snapped. She became blinded by fear and enraged with anger. She had enough of his abuse, enough of his torture and enough of him.

Judging by reports and some unofficial accounts, what happened next is still a bit of a mystery. According to her first testimony, Kathryn came home that night and the following morning found her husband naked on the side porch, beaten to death. Blood spilled from the orifices of his body, and his lifeless corpse was covered in more than 150 marks and wounds that Chief of Detectives Paul Rapport described as, "enough to kill two mules." A neighbor, Peyton Mathis, reported that after receiving a phone call from Mrs. Holloway, he rushed over to help. She told him on the phone that her husband was bleeding to death. He told police that he saw Dave Holloway's lifeless body, lying on the bed in a room inside the Holloway home. The room was soaked and splattered with blood, and it appeared that Dave Holloway had been dead for several hours.

As police looked further into this awkward crime scene, they found the murder weapon upstairs in the bathroom. It was a feather duster, roughly eighteen inches long and weighing less than half a pound. It was found lying on the bathroom floor, covered in blood, matted hair and skin. This was no doubt a crime of passion and possibly self-defense. Though Mrs. Holloway recanted her previous statement, she did eventually confess to killing her husband and was arrested, jailed and sent before a grand jury for the charge of murder. She claimed the act was self-defense, and according to the press release by police reporter Kathryn Windham, her husband's attempts to "love up on her" was what provoked his abuse when she denied him. Dave initially used the feather duster to beat his wife, but in doing so, she grabbed it from him and proceeded to give him a "merciless beating" as Coroner M.B. Kirkpatrick put it.

During Kathryn's trial, she testified to the abuse she suffered at the hands of her husband, and it took the jury an hour and a half to find her not guilty of the charge of murder. The murder and trial made national headlines and was a news sensation for several weeks after the event took place. Kathryn eventually disappeared after she was cleared of the charges. Some speculate she may have moved back to Jacksonville, Florida, where she was originally from. She simply vanished like a phantom and was never heard from or seen in Montgomery again. Years passed, and the Holloways' house sat empty until new buyers came onto the market. Eventually, the home was purchased and restored, and it was even featured on a TV show for the Home and Garden network. Over the years, stories about the home started generating attention when

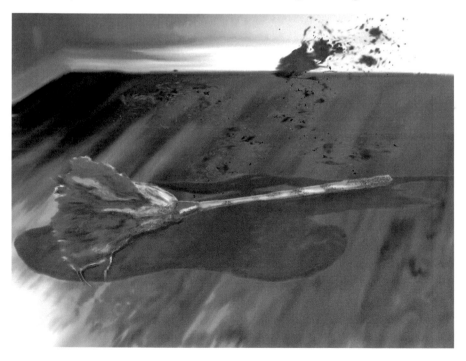

The murder weapon used to kill Dave Holloway was, curiously, a common feather duster. *Illustration courtesy of Brandon Stoker.*

spirits and phantom noises began to haunt the house almost constantly. Some of the tales have become the Garden District's most notable ghost stories.

Previous and current owners have reported hearing footsteps and the sounds of someone rummaging through the house during the day and especially at night. One gentleman staying with the family who owned the house at the time said he got up in the middle of the night to use the bathroom and bumped into someone in the hall. It was dark, and he was half asleep and hadn't seen who he bumped into. He apologized to his family the following morning for bumping into whomever it was that was in the hallway the night before. His family members informed him that none of them had gotten up in the night, so it couldn't have been any of them that he ran into.

The stories only get stranger from there. In the early 1990s, an emergency call was received from the old Holloway home about a possible burglary in progress. The responding officers came and met the homeowners, who informed them they were certain someone was in their home. Detective Shannon Fontaine accompanied them on the call since he was working in the area. Shannon was a homicide detective and formerly served in the United States Navy. He was used to being put into situations that were intense and potentially dangerous. The homeowners directed him to the upstairs bathroom. They were absolutely convinced that the potential burglar was held up inside. Shannon checked the home thoroughly and found nothing. At the time, he had no knowledge of the feather duster murder, nor did he have any indication of anything remotely odd in the home.

Several minutes went by while searching over the bathroom. Shannon knew there was no way anyone could be hiding in that part of the home. Suddenly, he was struck with an intense cold sensation. The overwhelming feeling of a presence took hold of him and he could not shake the sensation that someone was in that bathroom watching him. He instinctively pushed the anxiety into the back of his mind to stay focused on finding a perpetrator. However, not even his detective instincts could rid him of that unrelenting feeling that something was there with him. Though he sensed no immediate danger from the presence, it was certainly enough to stir him from the bathroom. The officers looked over the entire house and found no one inside, nor did they find any sign of forced entry. They reassured the homeowners the house was clear and left the scene.

Years later, Shannon approached a man named John Smith, a local attorney who lived at the old Holloway home. He confided in John his experience there while on that call back in 1993, and John informed Shannon that he also had a number of unusual experiences in the home while he lived there. At this point, Shannon had already learned about the murder but found no comfort in knowing that other people were experiencing the same things. Over the years the property has changed hands on numerous occasions. The address listed on the police report has now changed, either by real estate or by emergency services standards. The feather duster murder house is currently a private residence and is occasionally part of the Haunted Hearse Tours of Montgomery today. You can see this morbid curiosity from the back of Hilda the hearse if you book a ride. Just keep in mind that when your tour guide, a former detective who has experienced the home firsthand, tells you about his paranormal experience at the feather duster murder house, he's not telling you a ghost story—he's telling you a ghost truth.

THE BISCUITS STADIUM SPIRITS

Hordes of spectators from all over Montgomery and abroad pour into the Montgomery Biscuits stadium during the spring and summer for minor league baseball. Fans pack the stands for an afternoon or evening of good old-fashioned American fun. On occasion, a legendary player like Dale Murphy will make an appearance for fans that harmoniously line up and wait for hours for a chance at an autographed baseball or photo with the hall of famer. Masses of Biscuits fans collect their favorite ballpark snacks like, peanuts, hot dogs and cold brewed beverages and take their seats in anticipation for the game.

The sport of baseball has been a major part of American entertainment since the 1860s. It can be traced back to the early eighteenth century but was especially prominent in the 1920s and '30s, when legends like Babe Ruth, Lou Gehrig and Ty Cobb ruled the dirt diamond in the Major Leagues. Throughout the decades, baseball has changed dramatically, and today's minor leagues are riddled with the rising stars of tomorrow.

While attending games at the Biscuits stadium, you can pick up some great souvenirs in the team store, called the "Biscuit Basket." During game time, audiences proudly chant for the home team, "Hey butter, butter, butter!" a term truly indicative to the team spirit found here. However the team spirit isn't the only spirit associated with the Biscuits stadium. Prior to the stadium being built in this location, a cotton warehouse, owned by either Gilmer & Company or John Murphy, was used as a military prison during the American Civil War. This former cotton depot could hold as many as 700 men, and this facility held captive more than 650 Union soldiers for eight months between April and December 1862. Most of these prisoners were captured at the Battle of Shiloh (also known as the Battle of Pittsburg Landing), which took place in southwestern Tennessee on April 6 and 7, 1862.

According to archived records regarding the treatment and conditions of the troops at the Montgomery Military Prison, prisoners were kept in deplorable conditions. Captain J.J. Greer documented these conditions in his 1864 book, *A Yankee Loose in Dixie*. According to Greer, the cotton depot prison was only about two hundred feet long and forty feet wide. It was overrun with vermin and rodents. The men held captive here were given a sliver of spoiled meat and a portion of cornbread twice a day as their ration and often went without water. This prompted them to dig a well, and in doing so, they hit a layer of potter's clay, which they also made use of in creating items such as cups, pipes and rings. On occasion, they traded the items to Confederate soldiers in exchange for shin money (paper money with no real value).

Captain Daniel Troy of Hilliard's legion was in charge of the prison, and his supervising officer was Corporal Henry Wirz. Henry Wirz was and still is a well-known figure in the history of Civil War prisons. Wirz's ghost is also one of the most infamous and prominent of the Andersonville Stockade, also a prisoner-of-war camp located in Andersonville, Georgia, just north of Americus. Wirz was notorious for the awful treatment of prisoners and the conditions they were kept in. Whether it was on purpose or in retaliation for a lack of respect for Wirz by outranking officers, he denied prisoners medical treatment and sanitary environments. It's also plausible that Wirz's spirit is now trapped in a purgatory of his own doing at Andersonville, now reaping in death what he had sowed in life by the treatment of his fellow men during wartime.

Wirz's reputation at the Andersonville prison was cruel, and many of the captive men referred to him as "the Devil." Private Austin Car of the Eighty-second New York Infantry, a prisoner at Andersonville, wrote, "It is horrible to see the squalor and wretchedness here. Many men are fairly ate up with maggots and lice. The sight of a fellow prisoner in the agonies of death, excites no more feeling in the men than if they were watching an insect squirming in the dirt. It is a horrible place, a place of the living dead."

The conditions at the Montgomery Military Prison were very much like those of the Andersonville Stockade, if not worse. Records indicate 198 men died while captive at the prison. Most perished due to malnourishment and disease, while others died from injuries and infection as a result of denied medical attention and treatment. All these circumstances were preventable; however, in the primitive and dire stages of war, many of these deaths were inevitable.

On December 14, 1862, the Montgomery Military Prison was closed and the remaining prisoners were sent to Tuscaloosa. Those men who passed away while being held captive were buried in a section of the Oakwood cemetery that was donated by the city to bury the prison's dead. Some of the 198 laid to rest here were and still are marked, "Unknown." The rows situated in the northwest corner of the older section of the cemetery lay eerily silent. The gentle sloping of the hillside covered with military grave markers reminds one of the cost paid in times of war. The rolling marble headstones almost seem to bloom from the ground like the Cherokee rose that legend tells grew from the tears of mothers who lost their children during the Trail of Tears.

The cemetery may be the final resting place of a few of those men who died at the prison, but their souls are far from resting. The Montgomery Biscuits stadium is allegedly haunted by legions of soldiers still trapped in

Few graves from the 198 dead Union prisoners remain, but the reminder of those lost at the Montgomery Military Prison during the Civil War can still be felt.

their captive state. Many spectators have reported seeing the apparition of a skeletal figure lurking in and out of the areas near sections 101 and 102 on the ground level. A former resident of Montgomery took his young son to a game and met with players for autographs after. While walking through those sections, a strange shadowy figure appeared to be following them, but as the father occasionally looked back to see what or who was there, the shadow would dissipate and remerge once they turned away. The father stated, while interviewing for this story, "I don't know what it was. It was just very thin and shadowy. I couldn't shake the feeling that it was following me and my son."

These aren't the only reports of ghostly manifestations or unusual happenings at biscuits stadium either. During the off-season, patrons passing by the stadium while enjoying a stroll to the Riverfront district report the sounds of men screaming and weeping. Some have even been reported to local authorities as a possible crime. Officers arrive and find no evidence or indication that a crime has taken place. These screams and wails are believed to be those of the men who were imprisoned and died here in those awful conditions, still suffering in the afterlife.

Other supernatural sightings come from the constant presence of the spirit of a soldier who appears to people as a homeless man. Many have seen him, outside and inside the stadium, begging patrons for any food or drink they can spare. He never asks for money, just for necessities. If he is the spirit of one of the captive Union soldiers, money would be no good to him, so it makes sense that he would be asking for nourishment instead. Still cursed by captivity, this poor vagabond is never found when he is reported to stadium security, nor do authorities locate this paranormal panhandler outside the stadium. The spirit of this lonely and destitute soldier is somehow stuck in the realm of the living, still suffering in the realm of the dead. With no name and no way to understand why so many ignore and pass him by, except on occasion when the sympatric patron acknowledges him and offers him a handout, it's a terrible thought to know his soul may be trapped in that state for an eternity.

People of all ages will enjoy the American pastime of baseball at Biscuits Stadium for years to come, but be mindful of your surroundings. Lurking skeleton-like shadows and tattered and destitute spirits may be the last thing you'd expect to see at a baseball game. While going after that extra snack or beer during the seventh-inning stretch, remember to grab one more, as you may meet a very needy spirit on the way back to your seat.

THE WANDERING SPIRIT OF ZELDA FITZGERALD

Z elda: the name means "luck" in Yiddish. It's derived from the Anglo-Saxon name "Griselda." This name is also shared with a prominent character in novels about a gypsy queen that were favored by Minerva Machen. On July 24, 1900, in Montgomery, Alabama, "Minnie" (as Minerva was often called) and her husband, Anthony "Judge" Sayre, welcomed their sixth child, a girl, and named her Zelda. From birth, Zelda Sayre was doted on by her mother. She was seldom shy and saw no one as a stranger. As a youngster, she often found herself in trouble, even to the extreme of climbing into a neighbor's new carriage and nearly riding off with it at the age of five. She was an excellent student but was often bored and tired of following the rules in structured environments like home and school.

As she became a young teen, her craving for attention was immense. She attended social parties and dances and participated in ballets, which she loved above all else. As she blossomed into a young woman, Zelda was considered the prize of Montgomery. She was young, she was beautiful and her family was well established financially. Zelda was not the typical southern belle of the 1900s. She was interested in high fashion and standing out from the mainstream. While other girls who attended the same social gatherings as Zelda could be seen in graceful gestures of well-adjusted manners, Zelda was hanging out with the local boys, drinking and smoking and involved in very unladylike situations. Being the daughter of a judge was often difficult for her, and she found that her mother's leniency sometimes made it too easy to get out of trouble.

Zelda didn't consider herself easy or a pushover. She saw her behavior as a way to escape the doldrums of life and a way to be recognized for her rebelliousness. Rumors spread around town that Zelda swam in the nude in public. Her flesh-colored swimsuit was a popular topic in the summer of 1916, and her father actually forbid her to leave the house after the allegations became overbearing. Zelda wouldn't be denied her outings and weekend adventures, and she was quick to escape her room in the middle of the night from her bedroom window.

Pushing her luck, a wayward attitude and flamboyant ambitions may have helped her escape the confines of everyday life, but Zelda found pleasure in reading fairy tales and writing as well. She spent much of her school years involved in talent and dance shows but often participated in writing contests and wrote poetry. Her fondness of literature came from her mother, who also wrote and collected several short stories and novels.

In July 1918, just a month after her graduation from high school, Zelda attended a function at a local country club. She was asked to preform that night and, after, meet a young man named Scott Fitzgerald. Scott had recently moved into camp Sheridan the month before and was a first lieutenant in the Sixty-seventh Infantry. He was a bit older than Zelda, but he was immediately attracted to her. He was warned by some of his friends that she was a local high school girl and was told to be mindful of her reputation for being "fast." Scott wasn't interested in her reputation and made his way over to speak to her and asked her for a dance. Zelda recalled in a later interview that moment when she danced with Scott for the first time: "There seemed to be some heavenly support beneath his shoulder blades that lifted his feet from the ground in ecstatic suspension, as if he secretly enjoyed the ability to fly but was walking as a compromise to convention." There was no doubt a mutual attraction at the time of their meeting, but their relationship would grow to be an exciting but devastating experience for both of them.

To begin with, Zelda was not very interested in Scott's advances for a relationship. She had many other suitors all desperately seeking her attention. Fighting for Zelda's honor was common, and the local Baptist church had become somewhat of a battleground between young military men who all urgently sought to be her boyfriend. Pilots from nearby Taylor Field would do amazing stunts over her house at 6 Pleasant Avenue in an effort to amuse her, but Scott pursued her anyway. Zelda eventually became more receptive to Scott's advances once she realized they shared a love of writing. He had previously attended Princeton and was an aspiring writer who was working hard to become recognized for his literary works. His military career came as a result of the war, and his formal education was hindered on account.

Whenever Scott was free, he came to town to visit Zelda. They spent long hours together talking about poetry and romance, but Zelda would not completely commit herself to him. However, she did take advantage of the time she could with Scott and eventually invited him to dinner. Scott recalled the taunting behavior of Zelda that evening at dinner with her family and how he could never forget how she teased her father into such a fury that he chased her about the dining room with a knife. This was Zelda's nature and how she gained attention from people. Scott would have done well to be warned by this, but he found it amusing and continued his pursuit to win the heart of Montgomery's ultimate prize.

Zelda's family did not approve of Scott's Catholic upbringing, but in March 1920, Scott sent Zelda his mother's wedding ring and they became engaged. She agreed to marry him once his novel *This Side of Paradise* was published, and on April 3, 1920, Scott and Zelda were married in New York at Saint Patrick's Cathedral. Scott and Zelda Fitzgerald became celebrities in New York and were considered the faces of the age. The jazz era (also known as the flapper era) of the Roaring '20s had established itself as a time of casual social scenes and a time where woman were particularly changing the image of the modern female. Flappers dressed in short dresses in new-age fashion, wore bobbed haircuts with feathers and were decorated in flashy costume jewelry. This was not the typical image of the modern woman of the decades prior to the 1920s. In that time, it was customary for women to be polite and modest, to cover themselves from head to toe and to treat men as authority figures rather than equals. Zelda was already ahead of her time. She was never accustomed to modesty, and by the time the flapper era erupted, Zelda was leading the way.

Scott and Zelda Fitzgerald hadn't been married long when the problems between them started to arise. Scott was a heavy drinker, and so was Zelda, for a time. Scott's dedication to writing often left Zelda in solitude, and her natural ability to gain attention was displaced by his ambitions. Often the two could be found fighting in public. Drunken, violent altercations and arguments gained them a reputation as being very scandalous, and they were thrown out of both the Biltmore and Commodore Hotel's in New York for being drunk and disorderly. Zelda once jumped in the fountain at Union Square in Manhattan just for sport, but the couple was still perceived as prominent society, despite their alcohol-induced arguments and occasional unruly behavior.

Much to Scott's delight, in February 1921, Zelda discovered she was pregnant. Zelda, on the other hand, was not as enthusiastic about becoming a mother. She was not very domestic or maternal and was reluctant to give up her nightlife and glamorous parties. They planned a trip to Zelda's family home, where she would announce her pregnancy to her family and friends. While in Montgomery, Zelda took part in the annual *Les Mysterieuses* ball. The theme was a Hawaiian pageant, and Zelda gave the crowd a great deal of excitement when she danced across the stage in her masked costume and abruptly lifted her grass skirt, allowing the audience to get a good look at her backside. Whispers let out across the crowd that the masked dancer was indeed Zelda, making herself known in her typical unruly way.

Shortly after their visit to Montgomery, Scott and Zelda decided to take a trip to Europe before the baby arrived. While they were in England, they kept the company of fellow authors like St. John Ervine and John Lennox, the Irish playwright, and conversed with Lady Randolph Spencer Churchill and her son, Winston Churchill, who would later become the prime minister of the United Kingdom and who is also considered one of the world's greatest wartime leaders.

During their stay in Europe, Scott and Zelda debated on returning home for the birth of their baby but agreed to go back to Scott's hometown of St. Paul, Minnesota. Alabama was too warm, even in the spring and fall, and with Zelda in the later stages of pregnancy, she needed all the comfort she could get. On October 26, 1921, Zelda gave birth to a healthy baby girl. They originally named her Patricia, but her name was changed in a matter of weeks to Frances "Scottie" Fitzgerald. Little Scottie was tended to by a nurse, due to Zelda's postpartum condition and her inability to cope with the stress of a newborn. A few months later, Zelda found out she was pregnant again but, according to sketchy reports, chose to have an abortion, since having another child would ruin her figure and disrupt her lifestyle even more.

Scott's excessive drinking was increasing, and with a yearlong struggle to produce more published material, they struggled financially. Scott and Zelda both kept personal journals. Often, Scott would take portions of Zelda's diary to use in his own stories and novels. Zelda didn't seem to mind at first, but once Scott's novels began to gain interest, she became jealous and cantankerous. Scott's novel *The Beautiful and the Dammed* was published, but the debt they had acquired was vast. After he wrote a series of short stories called *Tales of the Jazz Age*, which helped to decrease their debt, they still struggled to live within their means as it fit into their lifestyle.

Zelda was proud of Scott and of little Scottie, but she was struggling to come to terms with her new state of anxiety and depression. These emotional issues were partially brought on by her feeling like she lived in Scott's shadow. Scott's excessive drinking was always a problem, and they left the United States for the South of France to live in the French Riviera with the hopes that some clarity could be found and that Scott could regain control over his habits and finish his literary projects. While living in France in a small villa, Scott was able to work harmoniously without the distractions and disruptions of Zelda. During the day, Zelda swam and lounged on the beach in relaxation but longed for a companion. She found just that in a young aviation pilot named Edouard Jozan. Jozan was nearly the same age as Zelda, almost twenty-five, and was devilishly handsome. As irony would have it, just like local air force pilots back in Montgomery, Jozan also flew his plane in acrobatic stunts near the Fitzgeralds' home in France in an effort to impress her.

Scott was happy that his wife had found a companion, but it didn't take long before rumors of Zelda's infidelity began to fly. Her affair with Jozan was short, and it is speculated that documentation of the event is included in her novel *Save Me the Waltz*. The popular belief is that Scott discovered the affair, and Zelda did not deny it and requested a divorce. Scott locked her in her room, and she slipped into a debilitating depression and overdosed on sleeping pills. Several different biographies later discussed the account as Jozan saw it. He reported that there was no affair, and the conflict between Zelda and Scott over the allegations was simply the need for Zelda to gain attention from Scott through drama.

While Scott's alcoholism got worse, Zelda's depression did as well. She developed colitis, an illness that causes inflammation in the lower bowels and causes terrible cramping in the abdomen. She began painting as an outlet while Scott was consumed in one of his greatest literary works, *The Great Gatsby*. During this time, Scott was introduced to American author and journalist Ernest Hemingway. While Scott and Ernest were successfully reestablishing Scott's writing career, Zelda again became extremely jealous of the time they spent together and even accused them of having a homosexual affair.

Toward the end of 1926, the Fitzgeralds returned to America and Scott took a job in Hollywood, California, as a script writer. There was great financial gain in this opportunity, and Scott jumped at the chance. While in Hollywood, as usual, Zelda was bored and often wrote to her daughter, who was living with Scott's parents at the time. According to Zelda's letters, there wasn't much to do in Hollywood except eat and take in the view, but what she didn't write to her about was the fact that she suspected that Scott was now having an affair with a very young teenage actress named Lois Moran.

Zelda's accusations of the affair fell on deaf ears to Scott, and her jealousy escalated into anger. Though she treated Scott's associates with respect and a pleasant attitude, in secret, Zelda was destructive and abusive in her arguments with Scott over the matter. She even went as far as burning her clothes in the hotel bathtub in a childish attempt to show Scott her anger toward him and Lois. After Scott finished his work in Hollywood, the Fitzgeralds moved east to Wilmington, Delaware. On the train en route to their new home, Scott informed Zelda that he had invited Lois to visit them in Wilmington. Zelda became so angry in the argument that she flung her diamond and platinum wristwatch Scott had given her during their courtship in Alabama right out the window. As time went on, they were both in very poor health, especially Zelda. She was now twenty-seven years old and was desperate to become a star in her own right. She considered painting as a career and began to write again. She published four articles and also enrolled herself in ballet lessons, despite her poor health.

Though illness and depression filled their personal lives, to the public, the Fitzgeralds were still in the good graces of society. Scott was invited to attend a formal speaking engagement at Princeton in February 1928. Unfortunately, there was much drinking involved, and he returned home in a terrible state of drunkenness. Zelda flew into a rage, Scott responded by throwing her favorite vase into the fireplace and she retaliated by insulted his heritage and calling his father an "Irish policeman." Scott violently slapped Zelda in the face, giving her a bloody nose. At this point, the distance between them grew. Zelda wrote more often and sold several of her short stories from *College Humor* to pay for her ballet lessons. She exhausted herself in the eight-hour-long ballet practices. This caused her health to get even worse, but she wouldn't ask Scott to pay for her lessons or be involved in her own ambitions. Zelda's relationship with her daughter, Scottie, would also suffer due to her problems with Scott. Their relationship was more like that of siblings than of a parent and child, and she longed to be more of a part of her daughter's life but found it difficult to be a mother and a wife.

Zelda traveled with Scott extensively for the next few years to Paris, parts of Europe and to North Africa in the winter of 1930. She had a number of psychotic episodes during this time, and on one occasion, while Zelda and Scott were driving through France, she grabbed the steering wheel in an attempt to steer them off a cliff. She was paranoid, and her body began to show the ultimate signs of mental and physical illness. She rarely smiled, and her shoulders hunched over like that of a woman twice her age. She was withdrawn, except for when sudden outburst of paranoia would set her off on anyone who might be unfortunate enough to witness it. Zelda's ballet instructor had also witnessed her unusual behavior. Her gestures, facial expressions and even her voice all seemed to imply that there was something very wrong with her. Sometimes Zelda's fragile health would induce fainting spells and she would become incoherent in awkward states of anxiety. She suffered from terrible night terrors and nightmares of demons and awful specters. It nearly drove her to the brink of another suicide attempt, and Scott would scarcely let her out of his sight for fear that she would harm herself or others in one of her states of hallucination.

On April 23, 1930, Zelda was admitted to a psychiatric hospital located in the outskirts of Paris. She was in an extreme state of paranoia and anxiety and slightly intoxicated. She relentlessly paced back and forth muttering to herself, "I should die," "It's horrible" and "It's dreadful." It was obvious that Zelda was suffering from an extreme case of mental breakdown. She was released on May 2, 1930, against the orders of her doctor, but she was later readmitted to another hospital in Valmont, Switzerland, to address her gastrointestinal issues. The attending doctors noted that her condition was not only physical but also deeply psychological and requested she be evaluated and sent to another hospital. She was released on June 4, 1930, and the following day she was readmitted to another sanitarium located just outside of Geneva, in Switzerland.

Les Rives de Prangins was the foremost established sanatorium of the time, more like a resort rather than a psychiatric hospital. There were tennis courts, gardens and a farm, and the staff lived on the property as well. Zelda was a patient at Prangins for fifteen months under the care of Dr. Oscar Forel. During that time, he noted that Zelda was suffering dramatically from mental collapse. She would withdraw from conversations and become terribly upset and excited over basic conversation regarding her illness. Scott wrote to Zelda's family and explained the situation and her hospitalization. Letters from Zelda's mother brought her hope and happiness for a short time, but Zelda and Scott still quarreled through correspondence, which eventually led Zelda to stop writing home and to Scott all together.

It was mid-June 1930 when Scottie came to visit her mother. Zelda's mental state was still greatly unstable, but she was determined to show her daughter she was well and confident. After Scottie's visit, Zelda broke out with a bad case of eczema that lasted until the end of October. She was prone to the skin condition in the past because of the medication she took for her gastrointestinal issues. However, she wasn't taking medication for that condition at the time. Her doctors speculated that the strain of her forced assurance to appear normal to Scottie was too great, and the nervous condition that Zelda had developed was now taking a huge physical toll on her as well.

In November, the state of her skin condition had worsened along with her mental state. She was often nonresponsive and lethargic; she daydreamed a lot and talked about what was wrong with her brain. Dr. Forel called on another psychologist who specialized in psychosis. Psychosis (in that time) referred to many symptoms experienced by schizophrenics, but according to the notes and evaluations of Zelda by Dr. Paul Eugen Bleuler, Zelda displayed signs of being a psychopath. She was extremely intelligent and was very knowledgeable in avoiding the consequences for breaking rules at the hospital. Zelda's constant relapses into depression and outbursts of unprovoked anger left both physicians baffled and concerned over her condition.

At the end of January 1931, Scott's father passed away unexpectedly, and he returned to the United States. While home, he made a trip to Montgomery to see the Sayres and discovered that Zelda's father was very ill with the flu. He also discussed Zelda's condition with her mother and explained the theories of poisoned nerves and the strange mental and physical aspects of Zelda's psychosis. Oddly enough, while Scott was away in America, Zelda's condition began to get better. At his suggestion, Zelda took part in more physical activities, like skiing when the snow was suitable. Her attitude changed, and her physical symptoms began to diminish. It had appeared that Zelda was starting to recover. The long-term prognosis of her condition at this point was that she would be able to function positively, as long as she avoided confrontations with Scott. Her inability to take a back seat to his success had long been a troubling factor in her mental stability.

After thirteen months of treatment, Zelda was released from Pragins, and together Scott and Zelda returned to Montgomery again. They purchased a home at 819 Felder Avenue, which is located in the Cloverdale district. Zelda began to write once more, but her bad eyesight hindered her a bit. Her weakened physical state also prevented her from painting and strenuous physical activity. She wrote several short stories for *College Humor* but found her lifestyle in sleepy Alabama very boring. Scott took another job in Hollywood, and Zelda once again found herself in a similar situation to just before her initial breakdown. She was working at great speeds and isolated herself in order to write productively. She withdrew herself from her family and frequently wrote to Scott with mention of her struggles in writing. She constantly referred to herself as a poor writer, and she struggled mentally with her inability to be creative. Her body had failed her in ballet, her fancy lifestyle of glitz and glamour had fizzled away, her crafty attempts to be recognized for her creative ability were failing and her husband, whom she loved dearly, seemed her greatest adversary at times.

Zelda was on the verge of another mental collapse. Her father passed away on November 17, 1931, and again her condition declined. It was as if all the sadness in her environment was empathetically projected through her. Her skin condition began to get worse and became chronic; she was not sleeping well and now struggling with asthma. Scott returned to Montgomery for a short time and saw that the condition of his wife was not improving. They decided that a trip to Florida may help relieve her stress and terrible asthma. While there, Zelda improved for a few days but was still struggling to sleep. She found a flask in Scott's bag and drank the entire contents. Shortly after, she became delusional and incoherent.

Scott contacted another psychiatrist in Baltimore at the Phipps Clinic in another desperate attempt to save his wife's sanity. Dr. Adolf Meyer was the head physician at the clinic and worked closely with Dr. Squires who was in direct and constant contact with Scott about Zelda's illness. Zelda was admitted to the Phipps Clinic and under care there, she began to follow a regular schedule every day that helped her reduce her stress and fatigue. She again started to write, and during her stay at Phipps, she wrote her own novel, *Save Me the Waltz*. Scott had struggled for over a year to regain his writing time due to setbacks from Zelda's condition. When Zelda wrote Scott about her novel and told him she sent it to his publisher for approval, he became furious. Scott's anger was not directed at Zelda's success in completing her novel but more at the material she used. She drew from accounts based on their life together, just as Scott had done in his novels. He struggled to contribute physically and financially to his own work since Zelda's condition required a great deal of his time and money. But from Scott's point of view, Zelda was able to write productively without complication or the distractions of a mentally ill family member. Scott's anger developed into a poisonous vendetta against Zelda, and this wasn't the reaction she had hoped for.

Zelda's novel *Save Me the Waltz* was more than just a personal achievement for her. Her doctors found that she had an uncanny ability to narrate her feelings through writing rather than talking about them. Scott's anger toward Zelda, even with the doctor's explanation, was unchanged. He remained in a constant state of struggle, trying to balance his work and Zelda's, even criticizing her at one point, calling her a plagiarist. This resulted in mixed emotions and yet another setback for Zelda. All she ever wanted was to be

Scott's equal and to gain the same reputable status that he had earned, but there was no constructive way to gain that between her mental instability and Scott's anger and furious drinking.

As time went on, Zelda became somewhat of a laughingstock. Her peers and critics mocked her novel, and she was regularly the butt of jokes regarding her mental status and her "almost" creative nature. Scott's health was also declining rapidly. An X-ray revealed a spot of tuberculosis on one of his lungs, and he began treatment for his ailments in North Carolina. While adjusting to the transition to Asheville, North Carolina, the Fitzgeralds often stayed at the Grove Park Inn. Here, Scott met Laura Guthrie Hearne. She was a fortuneteller at the inn, and she and Scott began an affair (unknown to Zelda while she was in and out of the psychiatric hospital). In 1937, Scott took work in Hollywood again and had another affair with a movie columnist named Sheilah Graham. During this time, Zelda was admitted to the Highland Hospital in Asheville, where she eventually dissolved into herself and rarely spoke to anyone. She made several more attempts to commit suicide but gave up the hope of being successful. She was slowly sinking further into the depths of complete and utter insanity.

When Zelda was under extreme duress, she would claim to be able to communicate with God; William the Conqueror; Mary Stuart, queen of the Scots; and the Greek god Apollo, but when she was away from Scott and his disastrous behavior, she would improve mentally and her stability was met with optimism by her doctors. However, the toxic relationship of Zelda and Scott Fitzgerald would finally come to a bitter and awful end in February 1939. While on vacation to Havana, Cuba, Scott was drunk and tried to break up a chicken fight and was beaten up badly. Zelda was returned to North Carolina to the Highland Hospital, and the couple shared only a few more letters before abandoning their love and never saw each other again. Scott eventually settled down with Sheilah Graham before his sudden death in 1944. While leaving a theater, Scott was struck with an odd sensation in his chest. He returned home that evening and planned to see the doctor the following day. He was standing in front of the fireplace mantel when he suddenly was struck down. He fell to the floor, and in that instant, he died.

Zelda did not attend Scott's funeral in Maryland but received many letters from friends and family of condolences regarding Scott's death. Zelda stayed in Montgomery with her family until 1946. She became very religious and again claimed her direct communication to God led her to salvation. She wrote often to her friends that they should heed the warnings of damnation. Her daughter, Scottie, gave birth to two children while Zelda was admitted to Highland Hospital, and she was absolutely beaming over the thought of being a grandmother. Zelda lived out her last days at Highland Hospital in Asheville, North Carolina. On March 10, 1948, a fire broke out in the kitchen of the hospital. Flames engulfed the facility quickly, and the fire was almost perfectly contained by the fortress like building. Locked doors and chained windows prevented any means of escape. The fire destroyed the women's wing of the facility, and nine women, including Zelda, perished in the horrible destruction.

On Saint Patrick's Day, March 17, 1948, Zelda Sayre Fitzgerald's body was laid to rest next to her husband in the Rockville Union Cemetery in Rockville, Maryland. One of America's most flamboyant, controversial and explosive couples of the jazz era had finally fizzled out, and a small band of mourners and spectators gathered to pay their respects and see Mr. and Mrs. Fitzgerald into the afterlife. Sleeping peacefully in the garden of the dead, Scott's soul seems to rest easy now, but Zelda, of course, does not. Her spirit is still roaming the far reaches of her former homes and favorite locations. The Highland Hospital was just one of the many locations rumored to be haunted by her ghost. According to local legends and paranormal investigator Sarah Harrison of the Asheville Paranormal Society, Zelda's spirit still roams the former hospital grounds. Stories circulate about phantoms that appear and vanish in misty and shadowy apparitions and of the cries and screams of those women trapped in the fire that took their lives.

Ghost tours in Asheville hosted by renowned paranormal investigator and researcher, Joshua P. Warren offer some insight to the locations of Zelda's alleged spirit. The Grove Park Inn is regarded as one of Asheville's most haunted locations, and the spirit of a "Pink Lady" is most commonly associated with a woman who fell to her death from the fifth-floor balcony to the third-floor court in the 1920s. According to the staff at the Grove Park Inn, there is some speculation that the Pink Lady could indeed be the spirit of Zelda Fitzgerald.

Zelda and Scott did stay at the resort-style inn in the mid-1930s, and according to Tracey Johnston-Crume, director of marketing and communications at the Grove Park Inn, it's likely the strange, glowing pink apparition seen and reported to her by their project manager during recent renovations could be Zelda's ghost. Tracey has had a few experiences with the spirit, and the $25 million renovation seems to be amplifying the level of paranormal activity associated with the spirit. When the project manager saw a woman dart from one room to another, he followed her and found the room that she had entered was glowing in a strange pink light. Though no harm has ever been associated with the Pink Lady at the Grove Park Inn, her playful manner does frighten the guests on occasion. According to Tracey, the spirit is most likely to approach women and children. Several reports from the parents of youngsters have been relayed to the staff about children making mention of the "nice lady" and how sweet this spirit tends to be.

Ghost hunters come to the Grove Park Inn from all over the world to get a glimpse of the resident specter, and she is most often spotted in the Vanderbilt wing, where it's cooler. The spirit of this unknown woman seems to like colder temperatures. This was also a common theme in the life of Zelda. Her ailments with asthma caused her a great deal of stress during the hot and humid summers in Montgomery, and her physical condition contributed greatly to her anxiety and depression. So the Fitzgeralds moved constantly to keep Zelda comfortable in the hopes that no physical stress would provoke her fragile mental state.

Zelda's spirit isn't limited to the location where she died or recreated, and she is also rumored to still be haunting her former school locations in Montgomery, Alabama. Children that attended the old Sydney Lanier School (currently Baldwin) have been very familiar with the ballerina ghost that haunts the school auditorium. Even the newer location of Sydney Lanier has had a few curious reports of strange and haunting music. During a state drama competition in the mid 1990s, Jason Ingram, a drama student from Smiths Station High School, was attending the event on a weekend. Jason and a fellow student heard the sound of ballet music softly emanating from somewhere in the auditorium. Since there were people performing at the time, the two students went to find the source of the music to ask that it be turned off since it was disruptive to the performance. They looked for several minutes to find a source and could not locate where the sound was coming from, nor could they find anyone performing in the competition that was using music as part of their performance. Students who have attended Sidney Lanier over the years have not only heard the haunting music but have also seen the spirit of the ballerina ghost there as well, dancing through the hallways.

The former home of Zelda, now at 919 Felder Street in Montgomery, is today the Scott and Zelda Fitzgerald Museum and has been a source of a ghost story or two regarding Zelda's spirit for some time. It was saved from being torn down in 1986 and has undergone renovations and construction to bring the home to its current working state as a museum. According to visitors and staff, Zelda's spirit can be felt almost everywhere in the house,

Sydney Lanier High School has moved since Zelda Fitzgerald attended school there, but her spirit still haunts both the old and new locations of her former alma mater.

and the museum's executive director, Willie Thompson, says that Zelda's spirit is as wildly active in death as she was in life. A former employee of the museum told Willie a story about an evening encounter with the spirit of Zelda Fitzgerald. According to her report, she was sitting in one of the many rooms of the museum that was used as an office. Inside the room, above the fireplace mantel, hung a painting of Zelda's childhood home. While working at her desk, she felt the urge to look up, and just as she did, she saw the painting over the mantel come off the wall as if something had literally flung it. It came off the wall with so much force that it landed in the middle of the floor of the very large room.

A hint of tranquil mischief is sometimes associated with a strange electrical charge felt by visitors, volunteers and staff at the museum. Zelda's playful nature in her early years mirrored her happiest moments when she and Scott first sparked the disastrous fire of their grueling but historical relationship. Zelda Fitzgerald is the epitome of the modern woman, strong, independent and eager to make herself equal in the inevitable "man's world" we live in. Though soft and vulnerable, she never gave up on her dreams. Her undeniable ability to charm her audiences, even through madness, is still a force to be reckoned with. She still, though more stealthily, spiritually

The Scott and Zelda Fitzgerald Museum was the home of Scott, Zelda and their daughter Scottie from 1931 until 1932 and is haunted by Zelda Fitzgerald.

converses with those she seeks out to entertain. Her unrestful spirit has no doubt spilled over into the afterlife, contributing to the stories that will forever be told about her and her love for Scott, her downfall into madness and her undead spirit that holds her greatest audience captive for all eternity.

OAKWOOD CEMETERY

In the busy ins and outs of Montgomery, there is a scenic and serene cemetery filled with ornate marble markers and regal and majestic monuments. It's beautifully decorated with Spanish moss hanging in the trees and dense vegetation that blankets the tombs of the dead. Fragrant flowering vines and ivy creep along the lattices of the markers and monuments, and manicured carpets of plush green grass cover the rolling and sloping hillsides. Here at Oakwood cemetery, the souls of Montgomery's past are laid to rest.

This cemetery's origins are somewhat unusual as it pertains to a traditional cemetery layout and design. It has several sections, including Jewish, Catholic and military, along with the family plots and traditional burials. In the beginning, Oakwood was divided. The property donated for the burial grounds was owned by John Scott and Andrew Dexter. Both men were founding fathers of Montgomery but started out in two different settlements. On December 3, 1819, Andrew Dexter's settlement of New Philadelphia and John Scott's East Alabama were combined to form Montgomery. Many acres for the cemetery were donated by both men, but when John Scott ran into some financial difficulty, he sold his property to Andrew Dexter, and over time, sections of the cemetery were added on.

The old graveyard, as the older part of Oakwood is commonly referred to, was a free burial location, and this added to its irregular and inconsistent layout. Many of the graves here are somewhat out of order. The aspect of segregated burial wasn't recognized at Oakwood, and many slaves were buried with the families whose plantations they worked on. Two slaves are recognized in the old graveyard. One known as "Jim," who was a servant to the Sebuessier family. His grave is easily recognized by the aboveground brick enclosure that marks its location. The second is Susan Tooley, who died in Montgomery in November 1856. She too was a faithful servant and is buried adjacent to Jim.

In 1918, there was an outbreak of Spanish flu that developed at Camp Sheridan and spread throughout Montgomery. Reports of death from the epidemic at Camp Sheridan are over two thousand, and many of those soldiers are buried at Oakwood as well. More than twelve thousand deaths in the city were attributed to the illness, and areas of the cemetery began to overflow with the dead. Records indicate many of the victims of flu buried here are marked as "Unknown." According to unofficial records, bodies piled up so fast at the cemetery that hasty and rushed burials made it difficult to keep track of everyone buried during this time.

Other unknown graves in the cemetery are documented by cause of death. Some of those graves are listed as such:

Unknown, infant, found in L&N yards.
Unknown, killed by L&N railroad train near Selma Road Overpass.
Unknown, found in well.
Unknown, found dead in J.C. Stratford's yard.
Unknown, died in jail, apoplexy, 1887.
Unknown, found in car at railroad yard, female, age 13, 1895.
Unknown, found in dying condition at the compress.
Unknown, cause of death, strychnine.
Unknown, cause of death, acute alcoholism.
Unknown, infant found in Catoma Creek.
Unknown, found drowned near the wharf, 1883.

In 2009, a vacant lot close by the Oakwood cemetery was being excavated for construction when workers uncovered nearly one hundred human skeletons. Originally, they were believed to be victims of the yellow fever outbreak from the early 1800s, but through investigation, it was found that these were most likely the skeletal remains from a forgotten paupers' cemetery that was in the area. There are still sections of the cemetery set aside for vagrants, homeless and destitute people who die in the city, but today they are better cared for and the remains of those found here in 2009 are recognized in the Children of God Cemetery section of Oakwood.

The "Children of God" section of Oakwood cemetery was formerly a forgotten pauper's cemetery. It was rediscovered in 2009 when one hundred skeletal remains were found here.

Adding to the significant military burials at Oakwood, many recognized and notable Confederate soldiers are buried throughout the cemetery and across the gulley into East Oakwood. They include Major General James Holt Clanton, who led a brigade of Confederate soldiers during the Civil War. He was gunned down on the street in Knoxville, Tennessee, after an argument erupted over a trial that involved the Alabama and Chattanooga Railroad. He was buried on September 27, 1871, in the Scotts Free section. Others include Colonel Robert Fulwood Ligon, who fought in the Mexican and American Civil War; General James Thaddeus Holtzclaw, who was originally from Georgia and a Confederate brigadier general who later practiced law; and Major Henry Churchill Semple, who was known as the "Pelham of the West." He was a Confederate artillerist from Montgomery who led Semple's Battery into a great deal of intense fighting during the Civil War. Also buried here is Colonel Tennant Lomax, who is considered Montgomery's Civil War hero. He was killed in action on June 1, 1862, at the battle of Seven Pines in Virginia but was promoted to brigadier general just before his death. These men all add to an endless list of Civil War heroes resting eternally at Oakwood.

Perhaps the most haunting here are the 750 Civil War dead. Row upon row of white marble markers, all in the traditional military style and many marked "Unknown" are buried here. A few were Federal prisoners of war who died at the Montgomery Military Prison. After the war, the Federal bodies were exhumed and sent to the National Cemetery located in Marietta, Georgia. However, a few that never made it home can still be found in the cemetery. Others are silenced by time and forgotten, but every year on Confederate Memorial Day, all these men are remembered. The nameless and faceless are all recognized as patriots.

Captain Abraham Calvin Caffey is among the profound military figures and military-affiliated people who are spending eternity at Oakwood. He was a successful black businessman who also led the Capitol City Guards in the 1890s. Also buried here is Brigadier General Birkett Davenport Fry, who was involved in the manufacturing of cotton at the beginning of the Civil War and later became a Confederate general. He died January 21, 1891. Colonel Robert Tyler was the son of American president John Tyler and also the Confederate Register of the Treasury. He died of paralysis in 1877. Benjah Smith Bibb was a supporter of the Confederacy for many years and was the first office holder in Alabama to be removed by Federal authority. General Crawford M. Jackson was active in a number of military campaigns before the outbreak of the Civil War and served in the Alabama legislature as a house representative from Autauga County from 1843 until 1845 and again in 1855 and 1857. He died in 1860 and is buried in the old graveyard. A Revolutionary war soldier is interred here as well. Reverend George Gray McWhorter was a planter and minister for over forty years. He is buried in the Scotts Free section.

Government and political officials from all over the state have also been buried here over the years. Nimrod Earle Benson was not only mayor of Montgomery in 1847, but he also oversaw the construction of the state capitol building. He, unfortunately, was a victim of the 1854 yellow fever epidemic that killed several people in Montgomery. He died at age sixty on September 28, 1854. Benjamin J. Fitzpatrick was a very accomplished man and governor of Alabama from 1841 until 1845 and a United States senator from 1848 to 1849 and again in 1853 to 1854. He was elected governor from 1855 to 1861 and died on November 21, 1869.

Perhaps the most noted governor buried here is William Oates. He fought in both the Spanish-American and Civil Wars, where he lost his right hand. His contributions in these wars were considerable. In July 1863, he fought at the legendary battle of Gettysburg alongside his Fifteenth Alabama against the Twentieth Maine at Little Round Top. In September 1863, he was involved at the battle of Chickamauga in Tennessee, where he was shot in the thigh. Oates fully recovered from his wound, and was a significant part of the battles of Cold Harbor and Wilderness in Virginia. On August 16, 1864, he received a serious wound to his right hand, which resulted in an amputation. After the war, he advocated heavily for the voting rights of African Americans and poor whites. He was a member of the United States Congress and governor of Alabama from 1895 until 1896, when he left office and continued to practice law.

Other government officials from Alabama and prominent men of political nature can be found throughout the cemetery as well. William Parrish Chilton, a chief justice for whom Chilton County is named for and David Clopton, who was a member of the United States House of Representatives from 1859 to 1860. After the war, Clopton resigned and became a Confederate congressman. Abram Joseph Walker was a chief justice of the Alabama Supreme Court from 1859 to 1865. William Lowndes Yancey, known as the "Silver Tongued Orator of Secession," was also a Confederate senator. Jack Thorington was mayor of Alabama from 1839 to 1840 and director of the Montgomery branch of the state bank. He was also a colonel during the Civil War. Anthony D. Sayre (also known as "Judge") was the father of Zelda Sayre Fitzgerald; he served as a Montgomery judge and died in 1931 of flu. George Goldthwaite was originally from Boston, Massachusetts, and served as an appointed chief justice of the Alabama Supreme Court in 1856. Henry Washington Hillard also served as a colonel in the Confederate army and as a United States minister to Belgium from 1842 until 1844. He was also a United States congressman, a minster to Brazil and a leading anti-secessionist. All these military, government and political officials definitely add to the achievements of Montgomery's history, but what about those darker historical figures?

No ghost story would be complete without the strange and haunting aspects of something more sinister. There are a few notorious souls that haunt the Oakwood cemetery. These people add a bit of unusual and, sometimes, charismatic and romantic elements to the history of the city and to Oakwood itself. John Schockler, a fourteen-year-old young man, drowned in the Alabama River on May 27, 1855, and an eerie warning on his wave-shaped headstone reads, "Stop as you pass by my grave here. I, John Schockler, was born in New Orleans the 22nd of Nov., 1841, was brought up by good friends, not taking their advice, was drowned in this city in the Alabama River the 27th of May, 1855. Now I warn all young and old to beware of the dangers of this river. See how I am fixed in this watery grave. I have got but two friends to mourn."

Alongside the now overgrown gulley at Oakwood there is a hidden vault that wouldn't be seen by the average spectator. This vault is built into a hillside and appears to be nothing more than an awkward-shaped slab from the road. This interesting tomb can only be accessed once the visitor walks down the slope in order to actually see the entrance. The legend associated with this hidden tomb states that if you approach the vault, knock three times and ask a question, someone will answer you. As odd as the legend sounds,

The grave of John Schockler bears an eerie reminder of his death: drowned in the Alabama River. Now his wave-shaped headstone tells the story of how he died.

the actual history is just as strange. The man buried here is Samuel Phippin Wreford. He was a successful merchant who worked on Dexter Avenue. The mausoleum was originally designed to hold eight of Mr. Wreford's family members. He was buried in a metal casket in the shape of a canoe. For what reason he chose a metal canoe is only for him to know. That secret lies entombed with Mr. Wreford forever. At some point, someone wanted to know, because his vault has been broken into repeatedly since his burial in 1866—once by his own son, who stole the diamond stick pin he was buried with. The bones allegedly were scattered about the cemetery, and the vault was eventually welded shut to prevent anymore vandalism.

The "gentleman thief" of Oakwood also has a foreboding mystery to his tale. James Chastaine was a very handsome and debonair young man from Eufaula, Alabama. He was a proficient dancer and had a certain charm about him that was irresistible to women. He attended the most lavish and prestigious balls and parties in Montgomery. His family was well respected, and no one would ever take such a handsome and finely mannered man to be a common thief. James had a dark side, though: he was severely addicted to morphine. This addiction drove him to steal from the prominent and distinguished families whose parties he attended. The story goes that James was living in a rundown hotel on North Court Street. He was desperate, and his addiction had driven him to commit a series of thefts. Adolphus Sanford Gerald suspected James was the culprit and followed him and caught him the act of burglarizing a local residence. When Adolphus ordered him to stop, James proceeded to escape, and Adolphus shot and killed him.

Adolphus Gerald was made chief of police not long after the event and remained at that position for twenty-seven years. James Chastaine was buried in Oakwood in his family plot in March 1881. The burial was conducted under the cover of darkness to avoid any conflicts. His family later disowned him, and allegedly the family members who were buried there were moved from the plot, leaving James to spend eternity in solitude for his unforgiveable crimes. For many years after James Chastaine was killed, on the anniversary of his death (March 30), a dark hooded figure would appear at his grave. Presumably a woman, according to those who saw her, she wore a long black dress and veil, too dark to identify her, and she would leave beautiful white and red roses on his grave, hanging her head in mourning for only a few somber minutes before drifting away and disappearing into the night. Years have passed

The Wreford Vault is hidden away at Oakwood but has long been the source of local legend. Knock three times on the vault and ask a question. The spirits within may answer.

since the gentleman thief's death, but on occasion the shadowy woman appears, bringing with her the roses she leaves on James's grave.

Another unusual burial story could be told about William Ludecas. "Billy," as he was known around town, suffered from dwarfism. In 1905, the stigma of dwarfism was an affliction that hindered many little people. Billy committed suicide at age forty-one, and he was buried in a full-size suit and in a full-size casket. Billy wouldn't spend his afterlife in the same stigmatized world that shunned him from society.

Perhaps more controversial and arguably more sinister is a small location near the railroad where very few markers can be found. This is because the forty-seven men who are all buried here were executed by hanging. During the days of public execution, townspeople would gather from all around to watch. It was considered entertainment and acceptable in that time. The families of the men executed were denied possession of the bodies, and this section was set aside for those burials. The few that are marked read, "Unknown"; however, records with the cemetery do indicate to whom those unknown markers belong. As a means of deterring any further crime, names of these forty-seven are kept confidential, except to living descendants.

Other superstitious and metaphysical factors can be found at Oakwood as well. Strange relics have been found in the cemetery, bottles that read, "New Orleans radiated water from Ireland 1837." This is believed to be part of an early superstition that water could be made available to the dead in the afterlife. Many early graves were lined with quartz bottles of water, much like the Egyptian tombs, presumably to be used in the afterlife.

There has been some debate over the years about the delegation of the spirits of Oakwood cemetery in Montgomery. People come from all over the world to see this massive collection of Alabama's most influential and historical people. Tours are offered here by storyteller and historian Mary Ann Neeley. Her insight brings life back into this garden of brick and stone. The legends exist largely because of those who chose to believe them. Still, over the years, more and more history comes to life with every cemetery tour and day trip to Oakwood. Ghost stories are the stuff of legend, but most have some origin where they start. From there, they continue to spread throughout time like bits of stardust that fall down on us. Some sparkle, some fade, but only a few remain in a story, resurrected in tales and verbal traditions and eternally resting in the memories of those who believe.

PRATTVILLE GHOSTS

BEAR CREEK SWAMP

Hidden within the deep, dark recesses of central Alabama, just outside of the Montgomery city limits, is a secluded dirt road just off Highway 14. This dusty path leads to a marshy remnant of an ancient swamp. Entering this moss-covered garden at any time, day or night, one might begin to let their imagination run wild. Frogs croak a strange serenade, and deadly serpents slither about the swampy forest floor. The black, cold waters reek with the stench of decay as earth's natural form of decomposition renders the woodlands a proverbial grave of rotting foliage. From forest floor to canopy, all manner of birds and wildlife congregate here to scavenge the swamp, and according to legends, several spirits as well.

Bear Creek Swamp is located in Autauga County, about twenty minutes north of the city of Montgomery in Prattville. The area is older than the state itself, being established in 1818, which was one year prior to the admittance of Alabama to the Union. Autauga County has a tremendous amount of Native American history associated with Creek tribes. The Autauga or Tawasa Indians that were located here were a part of the Creek Confederacy and were descendants of the Alibamu natives who had inhabited the region for thousands of years and are also among Alabama's most ancient tribes. In fact, the state of Alabama was named after this native tribe.

In the chronicles of Spanish explorer Hernando de Soto, the Alibamus were documented as early as the mid-1500s and again in 1700 when French explorers discovered them living along the banks of the Coosa and Tallapoosa Rivers. Later, these French explorers would organize trade routes

The Bear Creek Swamp has a long and mysterious history that dates back to archaic times, long before Alabama was a state or territory.

within the Creek territories and more French settlers began to move into the area. This essentially led to the fortification of Fort Toulouse, which was overseen by Fort Jackson (in Wetumpka, Alabama) to protect French traders from the hostilities that were brewing between the Creeks and the impending white population in the early 1800s.

The majority of the Creek tribes in this region were lost and forced to relocate after the treaty of Fort Jackson and the war of 1812. When General Andrew Jackson drove out the remaining Creek natives, who were under the command of Chief Menawa at the Battle of Horseshoe Bend (near Dadeville, Alabama), it forced thousands of Creek tribes to surrender and relocate west of the Mississippi. Some branches of the Alibamu tribe can still be found in parts of western Mississippi and Louisiana today.

The forced removal of Native Americans has long been a facet in the oral history and legends associated with many tribes. Long before the settlement of Prattville or Autauga County, there were stories told of the magical wells and springs found in the Bear Creek Swamp. The spring heads allegedly had medicinal powers that healed the sick and cleansed the soul from a spiritual perspective. This led the Autauga to build their village in and around these sacred springs and wells. The village here was called "Atagi," which means "pure water," and the Native American stories shared from this set of Creek Indians are similar to many common stories still told today.

Some oral history from Caddo Indian legends, which also relocated into Mississippi and Louisiana, speak of a Great Spirit who rested harmoniously in a lush forest among the native people. One day a great dragon ravaged the land, leaving disease, hunger and devastation in its wake. These ancient peoples pleaded with their Great Spirit to relieve them of this terrible burden, and in doing so, the Great Spirit banished the dragon deep underground, where it would shake the earth and make the ground tremble, springing up wells of pure water. The Great Spirit reclaimed his resting place among the people of the forest, and it was considered sacred ground.

Because the location is said to be guarded by elemental forces, many people brave enough to venture into the swamp in search of these ancient wells may find themselves being stalked by unusual creatures and strange and haunting spirits. One teenage couple (now married and living in Montgomery) drove out to the swamp for an adventure. While hiking through the dense swampy areas, they saw what appeared to be a scantily clad and unusual woman crouching at the bank of the creek. When the couple saw her, they agreed she may be a person in need of assistance and rushed to help her. When they reached her, they both noted that she was very gaunt and her skin was unusually pale. Her clothes were torn and mangled, and her thin, white hair was matted and distressed. The young man reached out to touch her shoulder, and she turned with an awkward jerk. He stared at what he described as a skull-like face with fierce yellow eyes. The strange woman quickly rose to her feet and let out a deafening shriek as she flailed her arms about in panic. She ran swiftly into the denser part of the forest, and the couple ran after her, only to lose sight of her after a few hundred feet. They also noted at that point they could no longer hear the sound of her footsteps or her screams. They feared she may have collapsed from exhaustion and searched for many hours and found nothing. After leaving, they informed the local sheriff's department about what occurred. It is unclear if the local authorities followed up on the event, but neither of these individuals would dare step foot in the Bear Creek Swamp again.

A local hunter also confided that while on a hunting trip with his son close to Highway 14, a strange figure caught his attention in the dense wooded area in which they were hunting. The man had shot a deer earlier in the day and was tracking the animal's blood trail when it began to rain. He feared he may not find the deer but continued to look for it anyway. He came upon what he described as a white, mist-like apparition of a woman hovering near a creek bank. He also reported that his son saw the female apparition as well, and both were reluctant to approach it. He stated, "We just froze. What would you do if you saw something like that in the middle of the woods?"

According to legend, in the 1800s a woman whose name is unknown lost her infant child in the swamp and was never found. The woman allegedly died of a broken heart and in death still searches the forest of the Bear Creek Swamp for her baby. According to locals, one would only have to drive into the swamp at night, turn off the car and wait for the ghostly woman to come out. Apparently taunting the ghost of this woman works to a degree. Many younger generations of people say that if you stand alone and announce, "I have your baby!" she will appear.

Though many curious individuals and paranormal enthusiasts alike go to the swamp in search of these ghostly experiences, a few get more than they bargained for. There is apparently no shortage of paranormal phenomenon from the Bear Creek Swamp. Frequently, strange balls of light can be seen floating about the area at night. Most dismiss the lights as a natural occurrence like swamp gas, while others believe the lights are elemental forest spirits who guard the swamp and its many secrets, leading explorers away from the magic waters that are trapped just under the ground. Some have even speculated that these lights are the spirits of the Autauga people who were forcibly removed from their ancestral home or perhaps died in battle during the Indian Wars of 1812.

More recent accounts of ghostly sightings come from people who have seen the spirits of Confederate soldiers in the swamp. This is highly unlikely since Autauga was virtually untouched by the Civil War; however, those militia personnel fighting during the Indian Wars may be the apparitions that are seen. There were several skirmishes in the swamp between white settlers and the Creek tribes. Along with those are stories of people who have gone missing in the swamp during the pioneer days and during the establishment of settlements. More recent documented disappearances are on file in the county that attest to missing people last seen in or known to be in the Bear Creek Swamp. Occasionally, a few have been found, though not among the living.

Outside of the countless ghost reports, a few cryptic beings may also reside in this mysterious swamp. Most often, reports of supernatural occurrences coincide with a phenomenon known as "wood knocking," said to be a form of communication by Sasquatch (also known as Bigfoot). In Native American legends associated with Alabama, the Creek word "Honka" means "hairy man." Also derived from other Alabama tribes is the "Eeyachuba," meaning "wild man." According the tribal stories, both are supernatural creatures that live in the forest and are masters of camouflage and hiding. Some Native American legends even speak of the Indians trading and living alongside the humanoid-like creatures. Cryptic beings have long been a source of controversy, but it's believed among many Bigfoot hunters and followers today that Sasquatch is an actual undiscovered and undocumented species.

Regardless of the circumstances surrounding the theories, Bear Creek Swamp continues to be among the most recognized locations in central Alabama for its ghost stories and legends. It's better to understand the location as it has always been and still is today: a primitive forest with few inhabitants. Though encroached on and developed in a few areas, it is still hiding secrets in the murky and muddy waters, occasionally springing up the shallow wells of its mystical waters and reminding us that whatever magical powers exist here are protected by elements, spirits and even people. The Atagi people considered this swamp sacred; those who do not may be destined to experience the swamp in a terrifying way. Beware the Bear Creek Swamp!

THE CROSS GARDEN

Located on the outskirts of Montgomery, in Prattville, just off the main highway on County Road 86, is an unusual shrine and testament of faith. The Cross Garden is perhaps one of Alabama's most peculiar and interesting spectacles. It is a small section of County Road 86 that is littered with rusty appliances, wooden crosses and biblical verses. William Rice was the man responsible for the Cross Garden. It was his life's mission to share the gospel and the meaning behind his interpretations of God's word. He was compelled to caution people about the aspect of sin and what the Bible teaches regarding consequences of ill-mannered behavior.

William started the Cross Garden shortly after the death of his mother in 1976 and dedicated many years of his life to the concept of turning the majority of his property into a religious shrine. The eleven-acre location is full of rusty old household appliances scribbled with scripture and random pieces of square and triangular tin with religious statements, and on the roadside hilltop, near the main road, the skyline is dotted with the silhouettes of raggedy wooden crosses, some as tall as ten to fifteen feet. During the day, a peculiar feeling seems to drape over the Cross Garden, as if the plants and nature are slowly reclaiming it, but late in the evening and at night, the location takes on the characteristics of a true-life horror movie, giving it a very somber and eerie effect.

Many of the folk art crosses found here are accompanied by rusty metal signs with scribbled biblical verses like, "Read the Bible," "God said the world [is] coming to an end," "Repent," "You will die" and "Hell is HOT." They are not only meant to be warnings but also inspirational. Many magazines and books have featured the Cross Garden and Mr. Rice prior to his death in 2004. Rice felt compelled to teach people about salvation after he was saved on April 24, 1960. He was healed from a debilitating stomach issue that caused him to suffer chronic pain from ulcers for fifteen years. According to Rice, Jesus healed him, and at that moment, he was thrust from his chair, spit tobacco juice everywhere and started preaching.

William Rice also claimed that God spoke to him through numbers that represented many different things. His mother, for example, was born on April 27, 1905, and died on her birthday in 1976. This was a sign from God, according to Rice, and he commonly referred to his "mother's number" as twenty-seven. He also spoke of stories from the Bible, of the ten virgins, the eight men saved in the flood and of God's number, seven. This numerical symbolism gave him a spiritual connection to God and gave him an understanding of the messages he believed God relayed to him. Inside William Rice's home was an even more elaborate setting of crosses and images of religious art. "The chapel," as it was commonly referred to, was literally wallpapered with religious art. Every inch of

The Cross Garden in Prattville, Alabama, has been an oddity and attraction for more than twenty years.

Rice's home was packed and covered with images of Jesus and, of course, more crosses and crucifixes. Eventually, Rice had to move the display outdoors, working on the garden and adding to it for twenty years.

At the end of Rice's life, he was approached by what seemed like many writers, authors, media fixtures and more to tell his story before his time ran out. Rice was adamant about his faith and the meaning behind the Cross Garden. He was never seen without a crucifix around his neck or as a decorative accent to his attire, even if it was drawn on his clothes with permanent marker. Countless interviews relay the same information from Rice over and over. He never graduated from high school and frequently referred to himself as "not educated" but always followed with the reply, "I've got the best diploma in the world, from God, Jesus and the Holy Ghost."

His mission in building such an elaborate display of faith was a labor of love. Rice stated, "It was the hardest thing I've ever done in life. It hurt my chest. It's not something that people are used to seeing in a man's yard." And this serves true today. It still is not something people are used to seeing in a man's yard or on the side of a random country road. Still, the garden lives on and is survived and cared for by the remaining descendants of William Rice.

Opinions about the Prattville Cross Garden vary from person to person regarding the stories of supernatural occurrences that have taken place here. It's unclear if any amount of truth resides in the ghost stories from the location, but such a spiritual area should hold some form of other worldly power. Though Rice did not believe in an earthbound afterlife, he certainly preached about it and the possibility of burning in hell, depending on one's actions in life.

In one account, a couple was driving back to Sylacauga from Montgomery and had an experience at the Cross Garden that stayed with them both for many years. The young man had heard about the Cross Garden and wanted to take his girlfriend. He made a detour off the main highway onto County Road 86 in the late evening hours. It was August, and according to documentation, the night was unusually cool for that time of year. While driving slowly down the road, he pointed out the many crosses against the night sky. The couple was mesmerized at the sight of so many crosses and all the written warnings that adorned each one.

They hadn't gotten far on the road when suddenly they saw something moving against a rusty pickup truck. Its eyes were illuminating a vicious

In recent years, more reports of supernatural phenomenon have been reported from the Cross Garden.

red color, and they were both terrified until the likeness of a raccoon shot out from under the truck. It startled them both to the point of screaming. After the initial shock wore off, they collected their thoughts and decided it was best if they just left the scene. Just as they started to pull off, the car seemed to be hindered by some invisible force. It wouldn't budge. A few more seconds went by, and the two were debating as to why the car would not go. Suddenly, the car lunged forward, and they sped away as quickly as they could, not stopping until they reached a gas station several miles down the road.

Another interesting story comes from a couple who visited the Cross Garden on an outing while looking into haunted places in Prattville. They hadn't been at the garden long and were looking over the scriptures and reading the messages on the roadside display when an ominous sound started emanating from one of the rusty appliances. The couple described the relic as an old top-loading washing machine. The top had been removed, and just in front of it was a sign that read, "Jesus Saves." The strange buzzing sound was building in the old machine. Of course, there was no power to it, so how could that be? As they moved in closer to get a better look, the sound gradually got louder and louder, like the mechanical parts inside it were still working and functioning. Baffled and more than perplexed, they studied the washer more closely and looked inside carefully in case some creature or insects inhabited it.

The woman picked up a long stick that was lying on the ground and began to rattle it around inside the machine. To her surprise, the mechanical sound stopped almost as quickly as it had started. Her friend looked at her dumbfounded and rested his foot on top of it to give it a shove, and suddenly it began to buzz again. Fearing a hornet's nest was inside the machine, they were reluctant to taunt it further. They walked away a few feet and threw a small rock at the washer and again, the strange buzzing immediately stopped. This is uncharacteristic of angry insects, especially hornets or bees. Under normal circumstances, the insects would fly and most likely sting the perpetrator, but no amount of curiosity kept the couple there to find out.

The most recent account of potentially supernatural reports came in the fall of 2008 when people started reporting seeing a man in a white robe near the Cross Garden at night. As stereotypical as it sounds, many said the man had a striking resemblance to images of Jesus. As likely as it is to be a hoax, numerous reports from locals said they saw the man not as a ghostly apparition but as a real flesh-and-blood man. It's hard to imagine in today's society that Jesus himself would come back to such a cruel and daunting world, but if William Rice preached about his return and the damnation of his people through sin and purgatory, it's likely the message is clear.

> *For Christ also suffered once for sins, the righteous for the unrighteous, that he might bring us to God, being put to death in the flesh but made alive in the spirit, in which he went and proclaimed to the spirits in prison, because they formerly did not obey, when God's patience waited in the days of Noah, while the ark was being prepared, in which a few, that is, eight persons, were brought safely through water. Baptism, which corresponds to this, now saves you, not as a removal of dirt from the body but as an appeal to God for a good conscience, through the resurrection of Jesus Christ, who has gone into heaven and is at the right hand of God, with angels, authorities, and powers having been subjected to him.*
> *—1 Peter 3:18–22*

PRATTVILLE'S LADY IN BLACK

If you follow the Alabama River from metro Montgomery to the outskirts and into Prattville, Alabama, along the Autauga Creek, you will eventually find yourself within the reaches of the historic district located in downtown Prattville. Heritage Park is located just adjacent to a very large but prominent fixture in this historic landscape: the old Pratt Cotton Gin. This mill was once the site of the oldest continuously operating textile company in Alabama. It was the origins of Daniel Pratt, a New Hampshire–born son of a farmer, that established his hardworking nature and strict religious upbringing. Daniel Pratt established himself as a successful businessman in many ventures of early America. Some of his businesses included the manufacturing of cotton gins, as well as production of goods from flour and gristmills and cotton and wool from textile mills, and he was involved in the building of railroads during the Civil War. He also helped to establish some of coal industry around Birmingham.

During the 1850s, the Pratt Gin Company manufactured cotton gins and distributed them in many parts of the world. Orders came in from many different parts of Europe, England, South America and Mexico. By 1860, the Pratt Gin Company was producing up to 1,500 gins per year, and Daniel Pratt's companies had made him a wealthy man.

The mill and manufacturing industries of the pre–Civil War and Civil War era provided dangerous but necessary jobs for many rural Southern families. Children as young as eight were employed in these types of manufacturing companies, most often with their parents and siblings. Before the development of child labor laws in the early 1900s, many children employed in these mills were made to take on the responsibilities of helping with the maintenance of machinery. The ominous dangers of accidents were present constantly, and many children and adults were frequent casualties of millwork during this time.

The Pratt Cotton Gin was no different, and it, too, had accidents resulting in the deaths of many workers. Sometime during the manufacturing era of the Pratt Cotton Gin, a ten-year-old boy named Willie Youngblood, who worked at the mill, had fallen down an elevator shaft to his death. The building where the accident happened was called Gurney Manufacturing. It was destroyed by fire in 2002, apparently at the hands of an arsonist, and today it is an empty lot located next to the Picker House in Heritage Park. The topic of Willie's death has never been a sore subject with the town of Prattville, and it is a story that most people, including Mayor Bill Gillespie, are very familiar with. Mayor Gillespie was recently featured on an episode of SyFy Channel's *Deep South Paranormal*, where he spoke about the ghost of Willie Youngblood and how the story came to be.

The Pratt Cotton Gin, located in Prattville, Alabama, is the location associated with an infamous spirit known as the "Lady in Black."

In 1920, long after the time of Willie's death, people working at the old Pratt Mill started to report an unusual apparition. You would expect the culprit in this story to be the ghost of Willie Youngblood or at least a young boy, but instead, the spirit most often associated with this legend is a sad and solemn woman. Typically that apparition is seen dressed in black. From her head to her toes, her long pitch-black dress is no doubt the reflection of mourning. But mourning for what? The story goes on to tell of Willie Youngblood's mother. After Willie's death, his mother became distant and depressed. She visited the mill the day her son passed away in the horrible elevator shaft accident but could not come to terms with her son's death. Nearly a year passed after Willie's death, and she could not bear the feeling of sadness and loss any longer. She went down to the Pratt Gin Company dam, and with the water rushing violently over the concrete pillars, she flung herself over the dam and drowned in the cold, churning water below. She was so desperate to be reunited with her son that she felt the only way to see him again was through suicide.

The "Lady in Black" is now the spirit most often associated with Mrs. Youngblood. Because of her suicide, it's believed her spirit ventures through the locations of the old Pratt Mill, still looking for Willie. Her purgatory is a sad reflection of the outcome of such a traumatic and sorrowful event. It's reported and documented that the Lady in Black has been seen by as many as fifty workers at one time. This episode with the Lady in Black took place one afternoon when a woman was spotted on the second-floor spinning room, gliding among the machines. One by one, she looked over them and hung her head in a sad state. When workers spotted her, they were reluctant to follow. As she made her way through the mill, she glided down the stairs and corridors and into the mill yard facing the creek. The workers from the second floor all rushed to the windows and looked out only to see the woman glide effortlessly across the top of the water and into the center of the creek, where her apparitions then dissipated and could no longer be seen.

Another story came from a guard who worked the graveyard shift at the old mill. It was time to change shifts, and the new night guard was looking for the previous guard to clock in. He couldn't find him when he arrived and went to look for him in case he had fallen asleep in the guard shack. As the new night guard approached the guard shack, he couldn't see his fellow worker until he got right in front of the building. He looked through the glass door and saw him cowering in fear on the floor. When he approached and asked him what happened, the guard explained that he was conducting his nightly rounds when he met a strange woman dressed in black in the machine room. She didn't say anything but just looked at him with an expression of terrible concern on her face. He was about to ask if he could help her when she suddenly began to disappear right in front of him. He was so terrified that he ran to the guard shack to hide.

These experiences didn't stop after the mill was closed in 2009. Many sightings of the Lady in Black and her son Willie prompted the city of Prattville to seek out professional help to uncover more about the sightings of the ghosts at the old mill. A new team of paranormal investigators known as Deep South Paranormal came with an entire television crew from the SyFy Channel to gather evidence of these spirits and, not surprisingly, they did capture what they believe to be evidence of these supernatural events.

During the investigation, their ghost hunting equipment was "going off like a buck in ruttin' season," as investigator Keith Ramsey of Deep South Paranormal would say. Team members Benny Reed and Jonathan Hodges used REM pods in parts of the mill to get responses from the spirits. A REM pod is an electrical device designed to give off a static electricity field. If something moves into it that can't be detected by sight or sound, the device will light up and make a buzzing sound to indicate that some form of energy has broken the field. The theory behind the use of REM pods is that spirits can manipulate these fields, allowing paranormal investigators to document their presence.

Other devices used by the team, like the K2 meters (meters designed to pick up electric discharges), also responded by lighting up when team members asked direct questions to the spirits. Audio recorders picked up the voice of a small child saying, "Mamma" and a number of bangs and crashes with no natural source of explanation caused a few team members to be very uneasy. Hart Fortenbery and Randy Hardy, also of the Deep South Paranormal team, took on the unusual aspect of a voodoo ritual to provoke the spirits from their hiding place. Hart made "offering dolls" and while venturing down the Autauga Creek, toward the mill location, hung them in trees and focused his energy to conjure up the souls of Willie and his mother.

Evidently, the ritual performed by Hart worked. Later in the night, as Hart and Randy investigated the location of Mrs. Youngblood's drowning by boat in the creek, the remaining team members watched from the upper floor of the mill. To their surprise, a black apparition of what appeared to be a human-like figure manifested on the grassy patch of land located on the dam. The team captured the apparition on videotape and surveillance. Today this footage stands as the most credible piece of documented evidence collected in the case of Prattville's "Lady in Black." Mrs. Youngblood is no doubt still searching for her beloved son. His spirit may or may not be the one responsible for the EVP collected on their audio recorder that night.

It seems likely that at some point those two spirits would reunite and become a family again. Perhaps it's a matter of environment or a need for the conditions to change in order for the reunion to happen. The mill is currently preparing to become a residential location, and plans to convert the Pratt Cotton Gin into apartments are already underway. It's likely with the construction and change the spirits will become disruptive and perhaps even bothersome for some time, but it would be a wonderful feeling to know that with the renovations of this location, soon to bring new people and families together, the spirits of Willie and his mother could also be reunited.

BIBLIOGRAPHY

PRINT

King, Carole A., and Karren I. Pell. *Montgomery's Historic Neighborhoods*. Charleston, SC: Arcadia Publishing, 2010.

————. *Then & Now Montgomery*. Charleston, SC: Arcadia Publishing, 2011.

Landmarks Foundations. Montgomery, Alabama. *Old Oakwood Cemetery: A Brief History*. Montgomery, AL: self-published, 2001.

Merritt, George, and William MacEwwn. *Hank Williams the Biography Colin Escott*. Rev. ed. New York: Little, Brown and Company Hachette Book Group, 2004.

Milford, Nancy. *Zelda*. New York: HarperCollins Publishers (Harper & Row Publishers), 1970.

Smith, Holly. *Alabama Ghosts: They Are Among Us*. N.p.: Sweetwater Press, 2006.

Windham, Kathryn Tucker, and Margaret Gillis Figh. *13 Alabama Ghosts and Jeffery*. Tuscaloosa: University of Alabama Press, 1987.

INTERVIEWS

Fontaine, Shannon. Interview by author. Montgomery, AL. April 23, 2013.

Harrison, Sarah. Interview by author. Asheville, NC. April 25, 2013.

Ingram, Jason. Interview by author. Phenix City, AL. May 24, 2013.

Johnston-Crume, Tracey. Interview by author. Asheville, NC. May 8, 2013.
Kidwell, Eric A. Interview by author. Montgomery, AL. October 24, 2012.
Neeley, Mary Ann. Interview by author. Montgomery, AL. May 23, 2013.
Thompson, Willie. Interview by author. Montgomery, AL. May 22, 2013.

WEBSITES

Encyclopedia of Alabama. January 2013. encyclopediaofalabama.org/face/Article.jsp?id=h-1184.
GenDisasters. April 4, 2013. www3.gendisasters.com.
The *Herald*. March 2013. montgomeryhistorical.org/ConfederatePrison.
Lady Muleskinner Press. April 18, 2013. ladymuleskinnerpress.com/2008/11/wc-rices-miracle-cross-garden/.
Maxwell AFB. maxwell.af.mil/.
Weird U.S. April 18, 2013. weirdus.com/states/alabama/stories/cross_garden/index.php.
William C. Rice's Cross Garden. April 18, 2013. thecross-photo.com/William_C._Rice's_Cross_Garden.htm.

ABOUT THE AUTHOR

Faith Serafin is a historian and folklorist from Southeast Alabama. She has two previous publications for the Haunted America Series from The History Press, *Haunted Auburn and Opelika* and *Haunted Columbus, Georgia: Phantoms of the Fountain City*. She is the director of the Alabama Paranormal Research Team, a nonprofit organization of paranormal researchers and investigators dedicated to the study of paranormal science and phenomenon. She is also a correspondent for the Paranormal Odyssey, an online podcast based on all things paranormal. Faith is also the official tour guide of the Sea Ghosts Tours at the National

"I never met a ghost story I didn't like."—Faith Serafin

Civil War Naval Museum in Columbus, Georgia. She also volunteers for local school and community programs for reading fundamentals and education regarding the importance of historical preservation. Many of Faith's published information regarding haunted locations, ghost stories, tours and public ghost hunting events can be found on her blog and website: www.AlabamaGhostHunters.com.